BRISTOL CITY DOCKS

Bristol City Docks

A Guide to the Historic Harbour

Ivan Benbrook

With additional research
by
Jeremy McNeill

R

REDCLIFFE
Bristol

First published in 1989 by
Redcliffe Press Ltd
49 Park Street, Bristol 1

ISBN 0 949265 68 X

*The main text of this book has been set in Garamond 11/12pt
to a measure of 21 ems.*

Photoset, printed and bound by
WBC Bristol and Maesteg

Contents

The photographs are by John Trelawny-Ross

About this book

This book is intended as a guided tour of the Floating Harbour in Bristol.

The text is set out in named sections, some including an illustrated map showing the main features of that part of the walk.

The first section is a short history of the Port of Bristol and the making of the Floating Harbour.

The subsequent sections provide information and history concerning what can be seen and something of what can no longer be seen. At the end of the book there are further information listings. Although the commentary commences at the Cumberland Basin it is possible to start a walk from where ever is most convenient and use the book accordingly.

In the summer months (April – October), a walk around the docks can be cut short by catching the ferry which operates on a circular route between Hotwells and the City Centre. However, it should be remembered there is no ferry service during the winter (which can be a pleasant and quieter time for walking) and that the full walk is approximately five miles.

Of course, you can always read the book from the comfort of a favourite armchair.

The text also contains elements of a personal point of view based on the commentaries given, over many years, by the author while skippering the 'Tower Belle', the Bristol Packet's 1920's river boat that offers pleasure trips on the Avon and in the City Docks.

Introduction

Today it is rather difficult to see the River Avon, as it flows beneath Brunel's Clifton Suspension Bridge and down to the Channel, as a treacherous waterway much respected by sailors, feared by shipowners and responsible for the making and breaking of Bristol as an international port. However, this river has the second greatest tidal fall in the world, and twice in every twenty-four hours millions of gallons of water come pushing up the Gorge and would flood out the lower parts of the city were they not held at bay by the Entrance Lock and the New Cut – the latter being a tidal by-pass for Bristol's famous 'Floating Harbour'.

This meeting point of a natural event and man's ingenuity in containing it seems an appropriate spot to start an exploration of the docks which were described, in 1720, by Daniel Defoe as ". . . the greatest, the richest and the best port of trade in Great Britain, London only excepted . . ."

A Brief History of the Floating Harbour

The Entrance Lock to the harbour is situated at the far end of Hotwell Road and to stand on its massive pier-head, looking across to the Somerset side of the river and down the Gorge to the Suspension Bridge, is to understand something of the achievement of the Georgian engineer, William Jessop. By digging out a by-pass for the river and damming a two and a half mile stretch of the Avon he created the Floating Harbour by enclosing the largest area of non-tidal water in the country at that time – eighty four acres in all.

7

Before this work the unfortunate shipping in the Port of Bristol rose and fell with the phenomenal tide of the Avon, which, so John Aitkin in 1788 tells us, came ". . . rushing in with great violence and rising to a great height in this narrow river brings vessels of a considerable burthen to the quay of Bristol, which extends along the inner shores of the Froom and the Avon. Here at low water they lie aground in the mud, which circumstances together with various other difficulties are the disadvantages under which this port labours . . ."

Other difficulties! The place was a shambles. Ships, once they had struggled into the harbour, found a total inadequacy of anchorage. They were often damaged by the reflux of the tide. The place stank in hot weather. The harbour dues were outrageous and to cap it all there were prolonged delays in loading and unloading so that anything up to five months could pass between arrival and departure. In short, the second greatest port in the land was having a crisis. It was being choked to death by a lack of space, a lack of foresight and an excess of greed.

The Merchant Venturers, at this time responsible for the running of the port, were more inclined to invest their considerable profits in fine houses and social niceties than tedious harbour improvements. In fact, the only people to rise above the problems of the place were the local ship-builders who, out of necessity, constructed vessels robust enough to withstand the hazards of their own port and in doing so won the respect of sailors everywhere and the enduring praise invested in the saying "Ship-shape and Bristol Fashion" – an accolade the city has been pleased to adopt without too much consideration for its original meaning.

Despite continual requests, pleadings, accusations and occasional violence, the Merchant Venturers managed to ignore this chronic state of affairs until such time as their own purses were affected. Even then, it was not until 1802 that William Jessop's plans to create a floating harbour were finally accepted – fourteen years after original submission.

Although William Jessop gets the credit for the harbour as seen today it was his son, Josias, who did most of the work – the father by then being too old for such an undertaking.

In 1804 the Bristol Dock Company was formed and work commenced on the construction of two entrance locks at Hotwells. Then, between 1804 and 1809, the six acre Cumberland Basin, the New Cut and two locks leading into the Bathurst and Totterdown Basins were built. The project was completed on May 1st 1809 and the cost had risen, to the horror of the parsimonious authorities, from an original £200,000 to almost £600,000.

As usual with the completion of such massive undertakings there were more than a few celebratory dinners, the most colourful of which took place in a field near the New Cut where, with beaming munificence, the directors entertained the labourers to a feast of roast beef, tons of potatoes, six hundredweight of plum duff and a seemingly endless supply of 'Stingo' – a beer of brain-addling properties. The labourers were mostly English and Irish and by late afternoon it seems the latter had consumed more than their share of the potent brew. This resulted in much aggravation which was finally settled by a vicious brawl in Prince Street where more than a few skulls were cracked and the much-hated Press Gang was obliged to come to the aid of the beleaguered constabulary or 'Guardians of the Peace' as they were then known.

The following morning, with a thundering hangover, the Port of Bristol opened its wonderful Floating Harbour and the money men eagerly awaited a second golden age of merchant ships struggling up the Avon. It never came and the decline of the port continued slowly until 1977 when it was closed down to commercial shipping by an act of Parliament.

The Cumberland Basin

The Entrance Lock

At the bottom of Granby Hill, which leads steeply up to Clifton, there is a pedestrian fly-over that crosses the main road to Avonmouth. From here you can enjoy an excellent view of the Entrance Lock.

Designed by Thomas Howard and opened in 1874, it is 350 feet long, 62 feet wide and the gates weigh 70 tons each. It was built to replace Jessop's original Northern Lock. If you can cope with the traffic roaring beneath your feet, this is a fine spot to watch the sedate business of sand boats locking through or the more amusing pandemonium of the weekend flotilla of river cruisers banging about prior to a line-ahead excursion down the Avon.

By crossing the fly-over you can enter the lock area, cross the inner gates and see what remains of the original entrances to the Floating Harbour.

Jessop's Northern and Southern locks functioned well for almost thirty years, but by 1835 the condition of the latter was a cause for serious concern.

Brunel's Lock

The Dock Company called in a young engineer who favoured stove-pipe hats, expensive cigars and went by the colourful name of Isambard Kingdom Brunel. His recommendations were so drastic that the Dock

Company went into a state of acute apathy, a familiar condition of the times, invariably brought on by the need for financial investment in its own future.

It was not until the lock started to fall apart that Brunel was invited to carry out the work of reconstruction. In 1844 he observed ". . . the repair of that lock is a most serious business and will probably involve a very heavy expense. . ." Even forewarned,

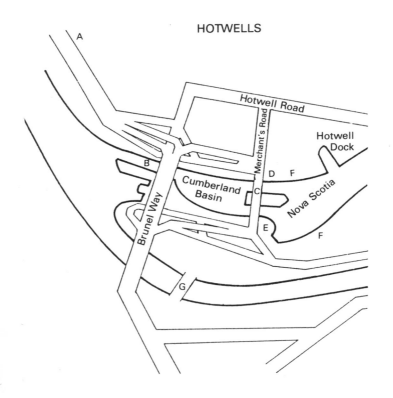

A: The Colonnade.

B: Entrance Lock.

C: Merchant's Road Swingbridge.

D: The Pump House.

E: The Nova Scotia.

F: Ferry Stages.

G: Ashton Swingbridge.

the Dock Company was stunned by the £22,000 estimate but now had no choice in a matter it had successfully ignored for ten years.

In 1845 work began on the building of a lock 245 feet long and 54 feet wide. It was a difficult job. The site was restrictive and shipping had to be kept on the move through the Northern Lock. Brunel managed to increase the length of the lock by the innovative use of single-leaf caisson gates made of wrought iron which became buoyant at high tide and thus easier to open and close.

It was not long before the reconstruction ran into difficulties. Many frustrating delays occurred and Brunel's relationship with the Dock Company eventually became little better than the state of their lock.

For one reason or another it was not until 1849 that the lock and swing bridge were in proper working order. You can see them both today – silent reminders of the conflicting attitudes to Bristol's future as a major port.

Time has proved Brunel right. The lock should have been twice the size. After all, he had already built the Great Britain, which, in 1844, stuck fast in the lock and was not able to get through until the coping stones were removed. It seemed obvious to everybody except the impervious Dock Company that ships were going to increase in size from the very day the Great Britain disappeared down the river, not to return for 127 years.

The completion of the Southern Lock, henceforth known as Brunel's Lock, marked the end of an era – that of the independent engineer seeking out commissions and almost heroic challenges. These romantic figures were replaced by the salaried professional – the sort of fellow whose sense of vision was encompassed by the parameters of his job, much to the relief of the tight-wads in Bristol.

Thomas Howard

Thomas Howard was Docks Engineer from 1855–1882. He is attributed with the idea of 'Dockization', a bold plan to make the whole of the Avon from Bristol to the Channel into a non-tidal harbour by building a dam at Avonmouth. The Corporation, who now ran the docks, were for the idea and the Merchant Venturers, true to form, were opposed. The issue was fought out in Parliament, the Merchants won and the docks at Avonmouth and Portishead were constructed in the late 1870's to accommodate the increasing number of ships now too large to get into the Floating Harbour.

Looking from Howard's Entrance Lock to the Cumberland Basin, Brunel's Lock is on your right and between the two is the bricked-up, mud filled, entrance to Jessop's original Southern Lock. Passing over all three is the Plimsoll Bridge, which was opened in 1965.

Samuel Plimsoll

This huge cantilever swing bridge is 250 feet long and weighs approximately 865 tons. It and the Cumberland Basin fly-over complex were designed to keep traffic on the move while allowing ships to pass into the docks. As is usual with such projects whole streets of charm and interest were demolished to make way for an improvement which, in this case, became unnecessary twelve years later when the docks closed down to commercial shipping.

Named after Sir Samuel Plimsoll, who was born in Bristol in 1824, the bridge seems a strange monument to the man who, when young, stood around these parts and watched grossly overloaded sailing ships leaving the harbour. More than a few such vessels, on meeting a heavy sea, would sink and sailors be drowned – but the owners invariably picked up the insurance money. Outraged by such callous profiteering, Plimsoll, when he became a member of Parliament, put through the Merchant Shipping Acts of 1875–6 which introduced the internationally recognized Load Line named after him and painted on the side of all sea-going vessels to prevent overloading.

Beneath the Plimsoll Bridge rests the swing bridge Brunel designed in 1840, using the technique of tubular girders made of wrought iron plates – a design he later used on his famous railway bridges at Saltash and Chepstow.

The Basin

You can walk all the way round the Cumberland Basin. Along the South side are the three monumental, red-brick bonded warehouses built by the Bristol firm of Cowlin between 1905-1919.

The North side of the basin was the site of the Foreign Animals Wharf which catered for ships carrying livestock into Bristol. Before the last war it was the delight of local kids to help drive the herds round the basin to the pens on the South side, or sometimes as far as the Cattle Market behind Temple Meads Railway Station. Occasionally the Roy Rogers element took over, causing something of a stampede, much to the anger of importers and amusement of on-lookers.

These days the Cumberland Basin, with the exception of the endlessly circling traffic, sees little activity.

Merchants Road, Avon Crescent and Underfall Yard

The Pump House and Junction Lock

From the Merchants Road swing bridge, which was also erected by Cowlin in 1925, you can look along the length of Howard's Junction Lock. On the left stands the Italianate Hydraulic Engine House, built by Thomas Howard in 1871 to provide pressure for opening two swing bridges and various capstans and sluices. It continues to function today, pumping beer instead of water.

You will also see, built into the harbour walls, what seems to be a pair of wooden lock gates. A second glance will show they are set in back to front. These are the stop gates and a very important feature in the workings of the dock when the big Spring tides cause the gates of the Entrance Lock to fall open and the Cumberland Basin to virtually overflow. Without the stop gates, which close automatically on these occasions, all this excess water would flood the docks before draining off into Bristol's basically mediaeval sewerage system, which would then back up, much to the domestic alarm of the citizenry.

In the busy days of sail the Dock Master, by closing the top gates of the Junction Lock, could use both the Cumberland Basin and the Entrance Lock as one, thus getting many ships out on the same tide.

The Nova Scotia

Heading right from the swing bridge you come quickly to the Nova Scotia, a pleasant pub standing on the side of William Jessop's Junction Lock, the only

original lock to have survived. Opposite is a row of
dock cottages dating back to 1831, and here lived some
of the men mentioned in the minutes of the Dock
Company meeting of April 1832 under the heading
"Wages for Dock men. Average wage for the fifteen
men being twenty shillings per week – some being
provided with Dock Company houses."

The Nova Scotia is a good place to have a beer whilst

sitting outside, perhaps reflecting on the forty-two year struggle that took place with the River Avon in order to give Bristol a modern harbour which would have been a great success had it not been grossly mismanaged by the Dock Company, the Corporation and the Merchant Venturers who collectively managed to scare away most of the shipping with a lethal combination of incompetence and cupidity.

Avon Crescent

From the Nova Scotia turn left and pass Howard's restaurant. Formerly known as Brown's, it is believed to have been the oldest transport cafe in the West Country. This was the departing point for the cumbersome, long-distance, waggons making their way to Exeter. Drawn by teams of six or eight shire horses, these impressive vehicles were the forerunners of today's heavy transport.

Now make your way along Avon Crescent where the houses date back to the 1850's and most of them still show the Port of Bristol plates above the doorways. Once round the corner and again involved with the traffic, there is a good view to be had by crossing the main road.

Ashton Swing Bridge

Looking to the right you can see the remains of the Ashton Swing Bridge spanning the New Cut. This work was completed and open to traffic in 1906, but only after much heated discussion as to how much the Great Western Railway Co should contribute to the total cost of £70,389. Originally a double-decker bridge, the lower section was used by trains and the

18

upper by carriages and pedestrians, who presumably disappeared in clouds of steam and smoke when the engines puffed their way across the river.

The length of the bridge is 582 feet and the original structure contained 1500 tons of steel. It was opened and closed by hydraulic power and the swinging section was 202 feet long and weighed 1000 tons. The bridge was made in Bristol by Lysaght and Co and remained in operation until 1965, closing down only because of the introduction of the Plimsoll Bridge and the Cumberland Basin fly-over. Whoever decided to dismantle the top section should be made answerable to the wrath of industrial archaeologists.

It is now best to re-cross the road and stride some one hundred and fifty yards until you come to the entrance of the Baltic Wharf Water Leisure Centre. Turn left here, passing the old timber-drying shed and continue to the water front. From here the view opens into a splendid panorama.

The Underfall Yard

To your left is the Underfall Yard, the long standing home of the Port of Bristol Authority's Maintenance Depot. The red brick buildings stand on the site where William Jessop dammed the course of the River Avon, and by doing so sealed off the tidal scour which had hitherto removed most of the sewage and other undesirable garbage of the 100,000 inhabitants of the City at that time.

The summer of 1825 turned out to be extremely hot and the harbour reeked to high heaven. Almost six miles of sewers drained into the water and the uncommonly high temperatures caused it to become 'a stagnant mass of putridity'. It seems that the only people unaffected by the dreadful stench were the august members of the Dock Company.

Nevertheless, it was not until a 'peremptory mandamus' from the court was obtained that the Dock Company approached William Shadwell Mylne. By 1828 he had greatly reduced the problem by constructing a culvert running beneath Broad Quay and Narrow Quay, under the harbour near Prince Street Bridge and into the New Cut close to the entrance of the Bathurst Basin. This work, while improving matters for the city, merely moved the offensive odours into more direct contact with those unfortunates who lived South of the Cut, and they had to wait another hundred years for the noxious business to be put to rights.

Although Mylne had rendered a great service to both the docks and the City, the harbour continued to silt up, and by 1832 the problem had become extremely serious. It was in this year that Brunel was first introduced to the Dock Company. When asked his opinion he promptly submitted a report which the company accepted, and in this way the harbour acquired the services, for the next twenty years, of the country's most brilliant engineer.

Under Brunel's direction a set of culverts were built into Jessop's construction at the Overfall, where the near stagnant water just about managed to flow over the top of the dam. By opening the sluices, which are still in use today, a powerful scouring effect can be achieved and thus, with impeccable logic, the Overfall Yard became known as the Underfall Yard.

The Yard, as seen today, is mostly the work of John Ward Girdleston, who was Docks Engineer between the years 1882–1890. He greatly extended the buildings here and then set about equipping them with an enthusiasm that was utterly repugnant to the penny-pinching Dock Committee who finally felt obliged to force his resignation for the crimes of "executing works without authority, exceeding estimates and purchasing plant without permission." It is with

The Underfall Yard.

The Underfall Yard: 'basis of impressive museum of industrial archaelogy'.

thanks to the impetuous Girdleston, who obviously had no time for the procrastination of committees, that we have today, stored in the Underfall, such excellent objects as a two cylinder horizontal steam engine built by Tangye of Birmingham in 1885, a Cornish boiler made by T. Beekey, a Feedwater Pump, a steam hammer, J. Whitworth's Slotting Machine of 1884, Shaping and Planing machines, and a hydraulic Testing Unit, all of which, one hopes, will form the basis of an impressive museum of Industrial Archaeology – should it ever be opened to the public.

The Underfall Yard remains the maintenance depot for the harbour. It is the last proper working part of the docks and thankfully retains much of its original character.

Baltic Wharf

Clifton and Cliftonwood

Directly opposite, and tumbling down from the skyline, are the terraces and houses of Clifton and Cliftonwood which were fervently described in Arrowsmith's 1884 *Dictionary of Bristol* as "...a prospect of the Avon that opens up like a romantic vision. The wrinkled, creviced and moss grown precipices appearing, and the symmetrical rows and crescents of handsome houses are piled story after story like the Hanging Gardens of Babylon..."

The terrace on the skyline is Royal York Crescent, reputedly the longest in Europe. It was begun in 1791 to the designs of William Paty. Two years later he went bankrupt and all work ceased. Then, in 1801, the Government purchased the land with the intention of building army barracks on the site. The local residents were thoroughly alarmed at the prospect of their

The Sand Wharf, with Cliftonwood houses in distance.

gentility being disrupted by the presence of rude soldier boys and their opposition became sufficiently heated for the plan to be abandoned. The crescent was eventually completed in 1820.

Below the terraces of Clifton can be seen the dwellings of Cliftonwood tottering down to the Hotwell Road. From this neighbourhood came the 19th century water-colourist, Bartram Hiles, the first documented 'mouth artist' in the country. As a child he lost both arms in an accident but nevertheless went on to master his art by holding a paint brush between his teeth. He achieved some recognition, eventually exhibiting at the Royal Academy. He was often to be seen around the docks and took to announcing his profession by wearing a wide-brimmed hat, flowing cloak and flamboyantly floppy bow tie. It seems doubly unkind that Hiles' career as an artist was terminated by his teeth falling out.

From where you are now standing, or hopefully sitting, perhaps with another beer from The Cottage, a pub which used to be the Wharf Master's house, you have a clear view of Poole's Wharf, or Sand Wharf, as most people call it. The chances are good that the sand boats, Harry Brown, Sand Sapphire and Sand Diamond will be berthed. These are the last commercial vessels to use the Floating Harbour.

The Timber Trade

The next section of the walk takes you past 'an exciting new waterside development providing 272 homes' – leaving one to wonder if the developer's excitement is related to the architecture or the prices, both of which seem questionable.

The new houses cover a site long associated with the timber trade in Bristol. Now known generally as the

Baltic Wharf the name encompasses a sequence of timber wharfs – Onega, Canada, Cumberland and Gefle. Lake Onega is not far from St Petersburg in Russia and Gefle is in Sweden.

After the completion of the Floating Harbour ships arrived here during the summer months, when the Baltic ports were free of ice. Their cargoes of 'great brown logs' were discharged from hatches in the bows and fell 'dashing and splashing in the water'. In 1860 the Water Bailiff reported he had found more than 2,000 pieces of timber floating in the docks between here and Prince Street Bridge, no doubt causing a considerable hazard to ships on the move. The whole area was said to smell of fresh pine – a pleasant change for these parts. Round-topped timber sheds stood where you now see the new houses.

There were no deep-water berths in this part of the docks and ships were obliged to come alongside platforms mounted on barges, or 'timber decks' as they were known.

Deal running, (the off-loading of the timber ships), was very hard work. Each piece of timber, and some were fifteen feet long, was carried ashore on a man's shoulder. By the end of a working day it was not uncommon for the men to find their skin raw and bleeding from the constant rubbing by the wood.

It was the steady refusal of the Dock Company to carry out any improvements here that caused most of the trade to finally move to Sharpness, where unloading was far less cumbersome.

The Docks Dredger

Making your way to the Albion Yard and new marina you will notice the culverts that are used to pump mud out of the docks and into the New Cut. You might even see the dredger, named after Sir

Baltic Wharf houses.

Samuel Plimsoll, at work. There is a bore at the front of the vessel which agitates mud and silt gathering on the harbour bed, this is then pumped out to the Cut where the returning tide theoretically sweeps it away down the River Avon. What actually happens is the mud piles up outside Thomas Howard's Entrance Lock and every time the gates are opened 70 tons of it comes back into the docks – thus making a sort of job creation scheme for dredgermen.

You will also notice examples of dockside enhancement in the three pieces of sculpture placed along the wharf. Commissioned at a total cost of £30,000 by the joint developers of the housing scheme to satisfy the planning department's requirement for 'value-added artistic embellishment', it seems extraordinary that the fountain held by Vincent Woropay's massive bronze hand does not throw water gaily into the air because the Engineer's Department refuses to accept responsibility for keeping it in working order.

Perhaps it was something of the same attitude which resulted in the decision to cover the embankment here with some kind of low-maintenance anti-personnel cement that neither man nor beast can sit or even walk upon. Apparently this alien matter is supposed to 'weather down' – but weather down to what? Flower beds and grass?

The Bristol Paddle Steamers

Before getting involved with the marina take a quick look at the newly erected boathouse, the home of the Bristol City Rowing Club, at the head of the ramp and to your right. The canopy of the roof comes from the old steamer landing stage, the remains of which stand on the Portway, just outside the harbour entrance.

Prior to the madness of weekend motoring it was popular to go for a Channel cruise on one of P. and A. Campbell's paddle steamers. In fact it was so popular that Campbell's owned eleven such ships with evocative names like Britannia, Glen Gower, Brighton Belle, Lady Moyra and Westward Ho.

Arthur Bower recalls that "all these vessels were

kept in spotless condition and the meals served in the dining salon were up to first class standard, served by properly dressed stewards and in the most courteous manner. On occasions the queues of people awaiting to board were immense and often many were left behind when a full complement had gone aboard. The return fare to Ilfracombe in the 20's and 30's was 7/6, (37½p)."

During the winter the paddle steamers were laid up at Mardyke Wharf, directly across the water. They made a fine sight with their raked funnels and highly decorated paddle-boxes. Today Bristol gets an occasional visit from the "Waverley", the world's last sea-going paddle steamer – a final reminder of an age gone and an elegance lost.

Albion Yard and ss Great Britain

The marina and Albion Yard started life as the New Dockyard when it was laid out by the firm of Hilhouse and Sons. In 1848 the company became Charles Hill and the dock was renamed as the Albion. The premier shipyard in Bristol, Charles Hill and Sons eventually closed down in 1977, apparently with full order books but unable to continue because of the closure of the docks. The largest ship built in Bristol, the 'Anglo', 3320 tons, was launched from here in 1959, and the last ship constructed was the Miranda Guinness. She was launched in 1976.

The three hundred-year-old tradition of ship building on this site is now continued by David Abel, whose company builds a variety of vessels ranging from work boats to pleasure trippers, including the charming 'Sutra', a steam launch often to be found moored in a corner of the marina.

Another interesting vessel based here is the pilot cutter, 'Peggy'. Built in 1901 at the village of Pill, on

the Avon, she is typical of the vessels that were often to be seen racing down the Channel, usually in competition with the Portishead cutters, to be first in getting a pilot on board a ship bound for the Port of Bristol.

You will notice the Yard is well packed with vessels of all descriptions, an interesting congestion mostly brought about by its no longer being permissible to take boats out of the water and place them on the quaysides. A few years ago you could wander round the docks and find an assortment of fellows repairing, scraping, painting or maybe just leaning against all manner of unlikely craft, each one a dream of journeys to be made and distant places to be reached. That most of them never got back in the water was of small consequence, for these endeavours represented something human and created an ambience around the docks that has since been removed by a corporate notion of 'tidiness'. So the amiable muddle of boat building on the quayside has given way to the blandness of 'sitting out' areas and wharves sanitized for tourism.

The Albion Dry Dock

In your wanderings between hulls and the heaps of jumble associated with them, this being the only part of the docks where boat-owners are now allowed to make a mess, you will eventually come across the Albion Dry Dock. It is 540 feet long and 43 feet wide and should be a major asset to the docks. Sadly it is rarely used. However, if the facilities of power and water were introduced and the berthing charges removed, this dry dock could attract more than a few interesting ships to Bristol for refits and maintenance – perhaps some would even base themselves here and gradually make the docks a national centre for those vessels that have managed to survive the breaker's yard – but old habits die hard and Bristol continues to retain a keen interest in harbour dues, regardless of the cost.

Walking round the head of the Dry Dock and down the alley on the left will bring you into Gas Ferry Road, at the far end of which you have no fewer than four options.

You can visit the Great Britain, whose masts and yards have been looming overhead for quite a while. You can wait for the ferry. You can turn right and visit the Heritage Museum, or you can take a guided trip round the docks on the Bristol Packet's narrow boat, 'Redshank'. If you are really keen you can do all four.

The ss Great Britain

To stand on the weather deck of the Great Britain is an experience to be highly recommended. This is not the place to give a history of the ship – the Great Britain gift shop sells an excellent one – but for those impressed by coincidence it is worth noting that the keel was laid down on July 19th. Four years later the ship was launched on July 19th. One hundred and twenty-seven years later she was eased back into the dock where she was built – on July 19th. No wonder sailors are superstititious!

Wapping Wharf

You will see the ferry stage on the way to the Great Britain. In 1853 there were six ferries in operation, each forming a vital pedestrian link between the two halves of a city divided by water.

Gas Works Ferry (you can see the remains of the gas works directly opposite the ferry stage), was established in the 1830's to take shipbuilders to work on the Great Western (Brunel's first ocean going ship), and later the Great Britain.

The Bristol Ferry Boat Company

In 1977 the City Docks Venture scheme restarted a ferry service. 'Margaret', the old 'Lamplighter's' ferry from Pill, was purchased and worked on a circular route between the Cumberland Basin and Bristol Bridge.

'Margaret' is still at work and now one of three boats run by the Bristol Ferry Boat Company, who took over the operation in 1978.

'Margaret' has been joined by 'Independence', a stout boat built in 1923 and recently featured in the Michael Caine film of Sherlock Holmes. The third boat is the elegant 'Countess'; built in 1896 she is the oldest working boat in the harbour.

The Ferry Boat Company offers a variety of services between April and October. Passengers can take a forty minute round trip of the docks from any of the ferry stages, or travel between any of the stops and on Friday and Saturday evenings public trips are available for a tour of the City Docks pubs.

'Independence' is not the only one of the three boats with a claim to fame. In 1976 'Countess' had the business of carrying the Duke and Duchess of Kent, and little 'Margaret' was featured on the 28p stamp issued in 1984 to commemorate the Urban Renewal scheme.

The ferry boats are easily recognized by their distinctive blue and yellow paintwork.

The Maritime Heritage Centre

Turning right at the ferry stage you will immediately come to the Maritime Heritage Centre, which was opened by the Queen on 26th July 1985. The Royal Party made their way from Narrow Quay (the Centre), in the Royal Barge which arrived at Wapping Wharf

at 4.00pm where the Guard of Honour was inspected, a plaque unveiled and speeches made.

In order for Her Majesty to disembark at Wapping Wharf a flight of steps had to be cut in the harbour wall. This done it was then discovered that protocol allows for no more than nine inches of regal ankle to be shown to the public, so a wooden platform had to be inserted over the steps. The platform and flag-waving crowds have gone. The steps remain, now, and for ever, graced by the title 'Royal' to distinguish them from their more lowly counterparts dotted around the harbour walls.

The Maritime Heritage Centre is well worth a visit, particularly with reference to shipbuilding in Bristol.

You are now on Wapping Wharf and should the need for refreshments arise, the Maritime Buttery, originally built as a Port of Bristol Authority canteen, offers a pleasant atmosphere in which you can gaze at the murals painted by Nick Gregson, whose late father drove a vintage motor car to Brighton, and enduring fame, in the feature film 'Genevieve'.

The Bristol Packet

Formerly known as Railway Wharf, Wapping Wharf is the site of the last modernisation to the docks, undertaken in 1965. The first thing you come to is the office of the Bristol Packet, the premier pleasure boat company operating on the docks. For many years the office was in a 1910, Orton and Spooner showman's trailer, a familiar sight on the quayside since 1973. However, as the wharf is revamped for the tourist trade, the Corporation has given the company a new base in the form of a stone-built hut from Avonmouth Docks, where, for many years, it did sterling service as the janitor's tea shed and broom locker.

From nothing less than the 'Royal' steps you can take a one hour round trip of the harbour on the narrow boat 'Redshank', which was built by Yarwoods of Northwich in 1936. Well known for 'colourful' commentaries, the 'Redshank' will take you from the Cumberland Basin to Totterdown Basin and is quite the best and most informative way of taking a look at the harbour.

The Harbour Railway

Just past the new Bristol Packet office you will come across the Bristol Harbour Railway's new and rather uninspiring station. From here you can take a short train journey to Princes Wharf, near Prince Street Bridge, being pulled along under steam by either the Portbury or the Henbury, the latter being a 1937 shunting engine that worked continuously at Avonmouth Docks for twenty-seven years.

Wapping Wharf is surrounded by water – the New Cut runs beyond the buildings to your right – which might explain the unusual name of Spike Island for this area. The derivation of the name is unknown but might have something to do with the almshouses and seamen's mission which stood near Prince Street Bridge, a 'spike' often being the slang expression for such places.

Brandon Hill and the Cabot Tower

Making your way along Wapping Wharf you will see, to the left, Brandon Hill and on top of it, surrounded by trees, the Cabot Tower.

Built to commemorate John Cabot's discovery of North America in 1497, the foundation stone was laid in 1897. The 105 foot tower was completed the following year at a cost of £3,250, which was raised by public subscription. A flashing light at the top spells out B-r-i-s-t-o-l in Morse code.

That a memorial to Cabot should be placed on Brandon Hill is not without irony. In medieval times there was a spring dedicated to St Brendan on the hill – hence the Brandon of today. It is now generally accepted that St Brendan landed on North American soil some five centuries before Cabot, who, nevertheless, continues to get the credit – especially in Bristol.

Here is not a bad spot to ponder the story of John Cabot, perhaps over a cup of tea on the 'Wilclair', a River Severn motor-barge built by Charles Hill in 1934 and now a floating cafe with the memorable name of Nutt's Landing.

In an age when developers and estate agents are renaming one wharf after another with such evocative and more 'exciting' names as Ferryman's Quay, Smuggler's Wharf and Merchant's Landing, Colin Nutt, the proprietor of the old Wilclair, deserves a medal. The food is good too!

Cabot and the 'Mathew'

In May of 1497, a little ship left the Port of Bristol, sailed down the river Avon and from thence across the Atlantic and into the annals of maritime history. She was called the 'Mathew' and commanded by Zoane Caboto, or John Cabot as we prefer to call him.

Fifty tons in weight and less than sixty feet long, the Mathew, (named after Cabot's wife, Mathea), was a tub-shaped vessel with raised castles fore and aft. She had three masts and a rig that remains under debate.

Cabot sailed westwards, perhaps further than any European ships had ventured, and the journey was special because it was more concerned with exploration than trade.

At this time 'educated' people knew that the world was round. However, it would be naïve to think all of Cabot's crew assumed this to be a truth. Some of them would have had a fundamental belief that progressing too far greatly increased the risk of sailing right off the edge of the world – an alarming prospect they courageously faced.

On such a small ship the comforts would have been few. Cabot probably had a tiny cabin in the sterncastle while the rest of the crew occupied the dingy, narrow space between the main and spar decks – an area affording no more than four feet of headroom.

Little is known of the voyage because there are no surviving journals. Cabot's son, Sebastian, might well have ditched them. He certainly made no attempt to perpetuate his father's memory – indeed, it seems he did everything possible to up-stage him and until the 19th century it was commonly held that Sebastian, not John, led the voyage.

From a letter by Pietro Pasquaglio to his brother it is known that – "the Venetian of ours who went with a small ship from Bristol to find islands has come back

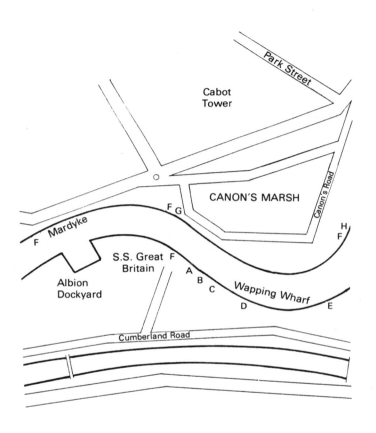

Park Street

Cabot Tower

CANON'S MARSH

Canon's Road

F Mardyke

F G

F

S.S. Great
Britain F

Albion
Dockyard

A
B
C
D

Wapping Wharf

H
F

E

Cumberland Road

A: Maritime Heritage Centre.   E: Steam Crane.

B: Bristol Packet Office.   F: Ferry Stages.

C: Docks Railway Station.   G: Gas Works.

D: Nutt's Landing.   H: Lochiel.

and says he has discovered mainland 700 leagues away, (a league being somewhat less than four miles), which is the country of the Grand Khan, and that he landed and did not see any person; but he has brought here to the King certain snares which were spread to take game and a needle for making nets. The King is much pleased with this . . . and has given him money that he may have a good time and he is with his Venetian wife and sons at Bristol. He is called the Great Admiral and he goes dressed in silk, and these English run after him like mad. . ."

In 1498 Cabot set sail with five ships. A storm struck and he was heard of no more.

Bristolians are particularly staunch in their belief that the name of the new continent comes from the merchant and harbour official, Richard Amerycke (or Ap Meyrick, Ap meaning son of in Welsh), who was a friend and patron of Cabot's, but there seems little to support this claim.

Continuing along Wapping Wharf you next come across 'Brunel's Buttery' where, particularly during the winter months, much dockside gossip is to be heard from the hunched figures of 'old salts' gathered round the outside tables. Just beyond the 'Buttery' are some public toilets.

The Fairbairn Steam Crane

Your next discovery is the wonderful Fairbairn Steam Crane. In the 1870's the docks underwent numerous improvements. At that time there were only 17 cranes throughout the harbour, none of which could lift more than three tons. The Fairbairn crane was ordered from Stothert and Pitt, the heavy engineers based in Bath, in 1875. At a cost of £3,600 it was operational in August 1878. The crane has a lift capacity of 35 tons. The curved jib has a radius of 35

feet, a height of 40 feet and extends 15 feet below
ground level in a metal well. The boiler was originally
fed with water straight from the dock. The cab remains
almost unchanged and close inspection will reveal the
only decoration on the crane in the form of small roses
cast into the interstices of the window frames.

The main advantage of the Fairbairn design was the
jib being able to reach well over the centre of a ship's

41

hold. The simple dockside crane tended to foul the side of a ship and could not lift loads from the centre or far side of the hold. Yet for all its advantages the crane has done little work in its life. A team of volunteers from the Industrial Museum is currently restoring it to full working order.

Prince's Wharf

Pressing on you come to Prince's Wharf, the home of the Bristol Industrial Museum and the National Lifeboat Museum. Both are well worth a visit and are housed in the old Prince's Wharf Transit shed which was built in 1951 to replace the pre-war granary flattened during the heavy bombing raid of January 6th, 1941.

You are now surrounded by cranes, steam engines and rolling stock. The cranes were built in 1952 by Stothert and Pitt. They were electrically operated and moved up and down the quay on tracks.

This is a very busy part of the docks today and at the time of writing there are some interesting vessels moored here.

The steam tug 'Mayflower'

Among them you will find the 'Mayflower'. She was built by Stothert and Marten at a cost of £1,000 and launched at Hotwells in May 1861. She is the oldest Bristol-built ship afloat and the oldest steam tug in the world.

The advantages of tugs were soon apparent in the 1860's. A sixty-five per cent saving was made on the cost of towing vessels by horse and speed was significantly increased – so significantly that there were numerous complaints from those left bobbing about in the wake.

The 'Mayflower' worked between Sharpness and Gloucester for many years and after modifications in 1909 expanded her territory from Worcester to Portishead. She was crewed by a skipper, an engine driver and the ubiquitous 'boy' who seems to turn up on all working boats.

In 1948 the British Waterways Board took control of the canals and 'modernized' the fleet by scrapping most of the tugs and installing diesel engines in the rest. 'Mayflower' survived because she was considered too old to be bothered about. However, in the severe winter of 1962–3, when the canal froze and the 'modern' diesels had difficulty working, she was again to be seen towing ships. Finally the British Waterways Board sold her for scrap. For another fourteen years she quietly rusted away at her moorings in Gloucester Docks. In 1981 Bristol City Museum and Art Gallery purchased her and she was towed back to the harbour one hundred and twenty years after being launched here.

It has taken six years for a team of volunteers to restore 'Mayflower' to her original working order and in the summer months she is often to be seen carrying vistors around the docks under steam.

The 'Pascual Flores'

A little further up Prince's Wharf, usually in the corner of the dock by Prince Street Bridge, is the 'Pascual Flores'. She was built in Alicante in 1917 and used to transport fruit from South America to Spain. A fore and aft rigged schooner, she was said to be the fastest sailing ship in the Western Mediterranean. She is now being restored as a sail training vessel by the Nova Trust and it is hoped she will be in commission by 1989. She might be a familiar sight to fans of the

'Onedin Line' television series in which she starred under the command of 'Cap'n' Baines. In Spanish her name means 'Easter Flowers'.

Some three years ago the 'Pascual Flores' was in the Albion Dry Dock for several months and her presence there made for a particularly interesting and timeless sight.

The 'Great Western'

Where you are now standing used to be known as Patterson's Yard, and it was here, at five minutes past ten on the morning of July 19th, 1837, before a cheering, flag-waving crowd of 50,000 that the ss 'Great Western' was launched. Within the hour of her entering the water there was the usual celebratory beano for three hundred dignitaries held within the hull.

The 'Great Western' was Brunel's first ocean-going passenger ship and a logical extension to the Great Western Railway. Travellers could take a train from Paddington to Bristol and then sail on to New York. It was the beginning of the modern world and the cost of an Atlantic crossing was thirty-five guineas.

During her eight years on the New York run she made forty-five voyages, averaging fifteen days out and thirteen days homewards. In 1847 she was sold for £24,750 to the West India Royal Mail Steam Packet Company whom she served for ten years before being sold to shipbreakers at Vauxhall, on the Thames. Nothing of her remains.

Prince Street Bridge and Bathurst Basin

At Prince Street Bridge you have the choice of continuing the walk to Bristol Bridge or making your way to the City Centre. The map shows the options and durations of the walks. The commentary, however, continues in the direction of the Bathurst Basin and St Mary Redcliffe.

The present day Prince Street Bridge was built in 1879. It is hydraulically operated and the swing section weighs 170 tons. The bridge has its own accumulator housed in the pretty, timber-clad, Italianate tower which provides the necessary pressure to lift the whole structure some three inches from the block on which it rests; the bridge then swings upon its sustaining pivot.

Originally there was a ferry here. Known as the Gib Ferry, it was owned by the Dean and Chapter of Bristol Cathedral. When the Floating Harbour was completed in 1809, the Dock Company constructed a wooden, double-leaf bascule bridge, the tolls from which were shared by the Company and the Dean, much to the growing indignation of the general public, some 220,000 of whom crossed the bridge in a year and provided the owners with an agreeable income of £1,100 per annum.

Later the Great Western Railway acquired the passenger tolls and it was not until 1876 that the Corporation purchased the bridge, abolished the toll and three years later had the present bridge constructed at a cost of £8,000.

The bridge is in continual use and it makes a pleasant break to watch the faltering process of opening and closing – although not many motorists seem to enjoy the therapy afforded by this leisurely event.

Keeping the bridge to your left and crossing the

road, you come to Bathurst Wharf, renamed as Merchant's Quay, no doubt to lend some character to the extremely dull presence of Merchant's House which was built in 1983 and certainly should have presented a more interesting appearance for such a prime position.

Unfortunately the sorry building and the new houses on your right stand on the site of the Turner Edwards Bond and the handsomely canopied G Shed, both of which were demolished in the name of dockside development in 1981.

On your left you will see the 'Glevum'. Originally a Gloucester grain barge, the 'Glevum' has been converted to a studio and art gallery by marine artist Vincent Neave. There is an annual summer exhibition on board which is always worth a visit.

The Mud Dock and the Gib

Across the water you can see the Mud Dock. This is the remaining one of a series of small docks that were built around the harbour before it was made non-tidal. The advantage of a mud dock was that a ship would sit down on a flat bed of mud when the tide was out rather than come down on a rock-invested slope, as was often the case on the Redcliffe side of the river.

To the left of the Mud Dock is the Gib and the little hand-crane there is a reminder of the Great Crane of Bristol.

In 1774 there were fourteen cranes available, one of which was a "building erected on fourteen pillars of cast iron, called the Great Crane – a curious piece of mechanism constructed by the ingenious Mr. Padmore".

At that time most of the cranes around the port were erected by the Society of Merchants and leased out to the crane owners.

Just to the right of the swing bridge you can see the wooden structure of the 'bullring' where the ferry boats moor and where the Aylesbury ducks frequenting the docks have made their home.

The 'Hole in the Wall'

Stretching away up to Redcliffe Bridge is the Grove at the far end of which stands 'The Hole in the Wall'. Formerly known as the 'Coach and Horses' in the 18th century, this pub has a small extension measuring three feet by four feet that affords the occupant a good view of the quayside in both directions. Known as the 'Spy', it was from here that a watch could be kept for the approach of the dreaded press gang, that bunch of louts who, on a commission basis, abducted young men and drunks into service on ships about to leave the port.

It goes without saying that the 'Hole in the Wall' has long been associated with Long John Silver and the 'Spy Glass Inn' from Stevenson's classic novel *Treasure Island*.

The Bathurst Basin

Turning right you come to the narrows leading to the Bathurst Basin which was built as an alternative entrance to the Floating Harbour for shipping using the New Cut. The basin is constructed over the site of a millpond where the Malago joined the Avon. The Trin (Trine, Trym, Trim, Treen – there seems to be confusion as to name and spelling) Mills stood here, using the stream to provide power.

In 1872 the Bristol Habour Railway placed a bascule (lift) bridge across the narrows to carry the mixed-guage line from Temple Meads to Wapping Wharf. The foundations can still be seen. Next to the Ostrich

Industrial echoes amid waterfront housing: former oil seed mill at Bathurst Basin.

(yet another waterside watering-hole providing good lunches and a pleasant atmosphere for an early evening drink), can be seen the cutting and tunnel entrance for the railway, which was finally closed in 1964.

The peculiar 'designer' bridge replaces a swing bridge

that was removed in 1965. It was not a particularly attractive bridge but it had the singular advantage of working, which is more than can be said for the new one.

On entering the basin the first building on your right is the old Robinson's Oil Seed Mill. Designed by W. B. Gingell in 1875, its polychrome brickwork facade is a fine example of the Bristol Byzantine style of architecture. Behind this elegant frontage lurks a squash court, apparently unused because the sound of stressed executives energetically whacking a rubber ball around has proved disagreeable to other executives in the adjacent houses.

Continuing round the basin you come to the original and charming houses of Bathurst Parade and the Bathurst Hotel. Until recently known by the even more stimulating name of 'The Smuggler's Tavern', the hotel is now called 'The Louisiana' and while in no way looking like a Mississippi stern-wheeler, it does have an attractive verandah, which, when first constructed, looked out onto open countryside, grazing cattle and Somerset sunsets. Today one can sip beer from the same spot while contemplating the traffic struggling with the roundabout below.

On your left is the Bathurst Lock which leads into the New Cut. The lock was permanently blocked during the last World War because the harbour authorities were quite rightly concerned that bomb damage here could drain the docks of water, an event which would cause most of the harbour walls to collapse. However, forty-five years later it seems remarkably off-hand that the lock and swingbridge are still not operational.

The newly 'landscaped' quay on the south side of the basin used to be a busy sand wharf and it was a good sight to watch the sand boats manoeuvring alongside in such restricted waters.

The General Hospital

The General Hospital, occupying the third side of the basin, was designed by W. B. Gingell between 1853-9. The ground floor was used for warehousing and chandlery to help finance the wards above which were sited so that patients could benefit from the 'fresh and bracing sea breezes' blowing along the New Cut – which seems quite extraordinary considering the sickening smells that issued forth from this stretch of water in the 19th century.

Patients at the hospital had an alarming experience on November 21st 1888 when a schooner carrying 310 barrels of petroleum blew up with such a colossal bang that most of the hospital windows fell out and the basin was covered with flames as the spirit spread over the water. The captain, mate and poor 'ubiquitous' boy perished in the calamity, but a sailor on board, having been blown twenty feet in the air, fortunately escaped with no more than a fractured leg.

Should all this excitement result in a thirst, you now come to the 'Ostrich'. Twenty years ago this was a cider house, furnished with bus seats, lit by paraffin lamps and peopled by dockers with bulbous, blue noses. One is left wondering where they all went.

Midland Wharf to Redcliffe Bridge

Continuing past the 'Ostrich' and bearing right you will come to Midland Wharf – now known as Phoenix Wharf in recognition of 'environmental' improvements made to the area by the Phoenix Assurance Company.

This is an attractive place and on the quayside is a 19th century hand crane and Benjamin Perry's fine wooden boathouse.

The modern boats of the Bristol and Bath Cruisers Co run from this wharf offering a variety of trips including candlelit suppers around the docks.

Redcliffe Caves

You will also find, in the reddish cliff face which gives this part of Bristol its name, a grilled door leading into the celebrated Redcliffe Caves.

The excavation of the Harbour Railway tunnel in 1867 brought the caves to light. The local press made much of the story and speculation became so rife that even today Bristolians show a marked preference for fiction rather than fact. Smugglers, secret passages, underground medieval hospitals, slave traders and dungeons – all have been erroneously associated with the caves.

The truth is not without interest. During the 17th and 18th centuries sandstone was mined from here for the manufacture of bottle glass and the glazing of coarse pottery. Sandstone was also used for ships' ballast. As the mining continued caverns and tunnels were formed and the roof was supported, to the height of some seven feet, by roughly hewn pillars which gave the place a somewhat eerie appearance.

Later these caverns were used by King's, the African merchants, who stored ebony, palm oil and tusks in them – which probably gave rise to the slave trade rumours.

The Slave Trade

The simple facts of the 'trade' were that almost once a week a ship would leave the port of Bristol bound for the Guinea Coast, which stretched from Cape Verde to the Congo in West Africa. Some of these ships, considering the vile nature of their business, had incongruous names like 'The Brothers' and 'Laughing Sally'.

From Africa, with their human cargoes, they made passage to the colonies of Virginia or the West Indies where African people were then auctioned as slaves to the plantations. The final leg of the journey was back to Bristol with cargoes of cotton or raw sugar. It was a triangular trade and a good profit could be made from each stage of the route.

As the anti-slave trade campcign of the late 18th century gathered weight it became increasingly difficult to find sailors prepared to crew on 'slavers'. No less sensitive to the welfare of seamen in Bristol than they were to the natives of West Africa, the owners and skippers of slave-trade ships resorted to force and trickery in order to gather a full complement. In collaboration with inn keepers, sailors were often carried aboard dead drunk, or, unable to pay the credit that had been foisted upon them by the inn, they were confronted by the wretched choice of imprisonment for debt or a sea voyage on a 'slaver'.

Death and desertion were rampant. Out of 940 men who served on Bristol slave ships in 1786, 239 deserted at the first opportunity and 216 died at sea.

Nevertheless, it was in Bristol that the first steps towards abolition were taken. In the summer of 1787 Thomas Clarkson came to the city to investigate the conditions of the 'trade'. He was followed by William Wilberforce and by 1806, despite considerable opposition, the slave trade was abolished by a long over-due act of parliament.

On first seeing Bristol, Clarkson must have felt something of the sinister atmosphere that existed in the city – an atmosphere of guilt mixed with venality, for he wrote – " . . . On turning a corner within about a mile of the city, at about eight in the evening, I came within sight of it. The weather was rather hazy, which occasioned it to look of unusual dimensions. The bells of some of the churches were then ringing. It filled me, almost directly, with a melancholy for which I could not account. I began now to tremble, for the first time, at the arduous task I had

53

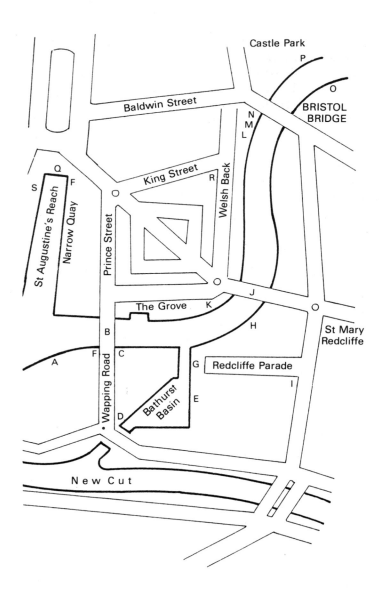

Castle Park

P

O

BRISTOL
BRIDGE

Baldwin Street

N
M
L

King Street

R

Welsh Back

Q
F
S

St Augustine's Reach

Narrow Quay

Prince Street

J

The Grove

K

H

B

A
F

Wapping Road

C

G

Redcliffe Parade

I

St Mary
Redcliffe

D

Bathurst
Basin

E

New Cut

54

undertaken, of attempting to subvert one of the branches of the commerce of the great place which was then before me."

It should please the reader to learn that retribution at least came to the 'Laughing Sally' in the form of a whale which attacked and sank the wretched ship.

Midland (Phoenix) Wharf owes its name to the Midland Railway Company which occupied the site as a warehouse and some traces can still be found of the rails laid for their wagons.

Plans have been afoot for several years for the caves to be made into a dockside 'feature' and opened to the public.

A: Industrial and Life Boat Museums.

B: Prince Street Bridge.

C: Glevum Art Gallery.

D: The Louisiana.

E: General Hospital.

F: Ferry Stages.

G: The Ostrich.

H: Redcliffe Caves.

I: Where the Shot Tower Stood.

J: Redcliffe Bridge.

K: The Hole in the Wall.

L: Loafers Sandwich Bar.

M: Tower Belle. (Public Trips from here.)

N: The Glass Boat.

O: Courage's Brewery. (Finzell's.)

P: Site of Bristol Castle.

Q: Neptune's Statue.

R: The Llandoger Trow.

S: Watershed.

From Midland (Phoenix) Wharf, you can either make your way to Redcliffe Bridge by following the quayside or by climbing the Donkey Ramp which will take you up to Redcliffe Parade. The ramp was originally used to transport goods from the wharf to Redcliffe Hill. Your short climb is well rewarded by excellent views of the harbour and city.

Redcliffe Parade

The Parade was long favoured as a promenade and vantage point, and there was a wonderful wrought-iron palisade with lamps that ran the whole length of the terrace. This most likely disappeared with much of the rest of Bristol's decorative iron work when it was removed as part of the war effort to assist in steel production. That it was ever used for this purpose is extremely doubtful and rumours suggest most of the iron work remains stored away in some corporation yard. If so, could we have it back now, please.

Redcliffe Parade is late Georgian and must have been a fine place to live when the harbour was full of sailing ships. Sadly most of the houses are now used as offices.

The end of the Parade brings you to Redcliffe Hill and a dual-carriageway full of roaring traffic. On the opposite side of the road is St Mary Redcliffe Church.

You now have the choice of visiting St Mary Redcliffe or bearing left and approaching Redcliffe Bridge, which will bring you back to the dockside.

But before doing either you should hear the story of William Watts who built the first lead shot tower in Britain.

William Watts and the Shot Tower

The tower stood, until 1968, a little to the right of the Colosseum public house, a pitiful building only receiving mention on account of its total lack of architectural merit.

Ever fond of a good yarn, Bristolians perpetuate the legend that Watts, too drunk to get home, settled down in the churchyard and, as is often the case with the deeply inebriated, had a nightmare in which his irate wife poured molten lead upon him from the church roof. The lead came down through the holes in the bottom of her rusty old frying pan and struck his recumbent person as solid, perfectly formed spherical lead shot.

It would seem Watts awoke an inspired man and, untrammelled by city planners, immediately dug out the basement and built a 50 foot tower on the top of his home in Redcliffe Street.

The shot making process worked and in 1782 Watts was granted a patent which, four years later, he sold to a London company for £10,000 – an absolute fortune in those days.

William Watts was obviously not a timid fellow for he decided to build the longest terrace in Bristol, which would start at the edge of the Avon Gorge, not far from the Entrance Lock to the harbour, and end goodness knows where. In order to get the massive project under way he was obliged to build a retaining wall on the side of the Gorge. Unfortunately this undertaking drove Watts to bankruptcy and an early grave. However, his wall remains and can be seen directly below Windsor Terrace in Clifton. It goes by the cautionary name of Watts' Folly.

Bristol still has a lead shot works. It stands by the dockside near St Philip's Bridge, looks like a tower with a concrete beer barrel on the top and, among other things, produces shot for a subsidiary of ICI who, as long ago as 1969, were producing over 50 million cartridges a year so that men might enjoy 'sport' to the detriment of wildlife right across the globe.

St Mary Redcliffe

The first record of the church opposite comes from 1115 when the 'Blessed Mary of Radclive' was given to Salisbury Cathedral by Henry I.

In 1190 Lord Robert de Berkeley donated land in the parish of Redcliffe so that a priest could live near the church. He also gave his 'ruge', or ridge, well to the church and had a two mile conduit constructed to supply it with water from Knowle.

Not long after the church was completed, the 'greate storme' of 1446 caused the tower to fall and do considerable damage to the rest of the building. Fortunately the illustrious William Canynge, who owned ten ships, was mayor of Bristol five times and a member of parliament twice, spent a considerable part of his fortune on restoration; however, the spire was not completed until 1872.

Inside the church is a large bone, reputed to be from a whale and brought back by John Cabot from Newfoundland. As though this were not strange enough, local legend claims that really the bone is the rib of the terrible 'Dun Cow' which, driven crazy by a prolonged drought, terrorised the folk of Redcliffe until the Earl of Warwick came along and slew the beast with a single blow of his broadsword!

In 1574 Queen Elizabeth I visited Bristol and lavished praise on the church by pronouncing it to be "the fairest, goodliest and most famous parish church in England". It is interesting to note that the prosperous company of Merchant Venturers 'borrowed' 40 guineas from the poor box to cover some of the expenses incurred by this royal visit.

St. Mary Redcliffe Church from Welsh Back.

Thomas Chatterton

The church also has associations with the poet, Thomas Chatterton, who was born in Redcliffe Way. By the age of five he was declared to be an unteachable dunce. Now regarded as a genius, even by some Bristolians, he castigated the city that rejected him with the lines –

"Farewell, Bristolia's dingy pile of brick,
Lovers of Mammon, worshippers of Trick!
. . . Farewell, ye guzzling aldermanic fools,
By nature fitted for Corruption's tools!"

In April 1770 Chatterton went to London seeking recognition but four months later, beset by frustration, malnutrition and disease, killed himself with a dose of arsenic mixed with opium and water. His body was discovered the next day, as were the ripped-up manuscripts which littered the floor of his room. He was seventeen years old.

The Bristol Quakers

Making your way down to Redcliffe Bridge you will find on the left a small walled garden. It was a Quaker's burial ground. The Quakers were heavily persecuted in Bristol during the 17th century; their meetings broken up and both men and women constantly fined and imprisoned – indeed, Quaker bashing was such a popular participatory sport in Bristol that it lasted for almost half a century and it is small wonder that many of these gentle people left for the colonies of New England, preferring hardship to ignorance and bigotry.

Redcliffe Bridge and Welsh Back

When you reach the large roundabout there is a pedestrian crossing which will take you to Redcliffe Bridge.

Redcliffe Bridge was constructed in 1939. An electrically operated bascule bridge, it was completed in 1941 as part of the disastrous Redcliffe Way road development which crosses the water here before crashing diagonally through Queen Square, the corner

Holiday time at Bristol Bridge.

houses of which were removed for this purpose by a totally unenlightened planning department.

After the bombing raids of 1940 and 1941, in which over 3,000 houses were completely destroyed and some 90,000 damaged, a pamphlet appeared from the Council House declaring that at least such wholesale destruction

The Old Granary.

created an opportunity to correct some of the building mistakes of the past – in the case of Queen Square we are still waiting.

We shall come to the history of Queen Square later in the commentary. Meanwhile, cross the bridge and turn right along the cobblestones of Welsh Back.

The Welsh Back

It is difficult to imagine the hubbub of this place some two hundred years ago. A contemporary tells us that about 1,300 vessels of various size arrived here annually and that the Bristol directories provided a timetable of the sailings of these vessels. The Severn trows from Bewdley, Bridgnorth, Frampton, Gloucester, Newnham, Stroud, Tewkesbury, Upton and Worcester left on every spring tide. The market boats of Caerleon, Chepstow and Newport arrived each Wednesday and departed each Thursday. A market was held here every other Wednesday when the Welsh boats discharged the produce of their country; fine salt-butter, poultry, roasting pigs and geese ready for the spit, apples, pears and great quantities of 'cyder' and here ". . . all are in a hurry, running up and down with cloudy looks and busy faces, loading, carrying and unloading goods and merchandises of all sorts, from place to place."

Of course, the area gets its name from the Welsh trade and there are some fine Victorian warehouses on your left, the best of which is the 'Old Granary'. Built in the style of Bristol Byzantine, it was designed by Ponton and Gough and completed in 1871.

At the end of King Street you will see the red-painted Lightship. A Trinity House vessel, built in 1936, it worked off the North-East coast warning shipping of navigational hazards. It has been in the docks since 1976 as a floating bar and disco. Immediately after the Lightship is the Bomb Hole, a reminder of the blitz in Bristol.

Continuing on towards Bridge Bridge you will find a couple of 18th century cannon that were found in the Albion Dockyard and from this area you can look across the water to Redcliffe Back. At some point in the future there will be a walkway on both sides of the dock, but at the time of writing the route along

The Lightship and, across the water, a superb warehouse conversion and 'new build' flats.

Redcliffe Back is interrupted by various developments that are still in progress.

If all this exercise has resulted in a degree of peckishness, the kiosk ahead, Loafers Sandwich Bar, will more than satisfy your needs and as you munch through one of their experiences you can cast an eye back to Redcliffe Bridge and take in the fine warehouses on the other side of the dock.

Redcliffe Back

The first, and most impressive, of the buildings is the old Western Counties Agricultural Cooperative Association. Completed in 1913 and an example of the early use of reinforced concrete, it has three handsome cantilevered bays. These are hoist-boxes and closer inspection would show the trap-doors in the bottom of each bay – thus shipping could moor directly beneath and cargo be unloaded straight into the warehouse.

The next two buildings are the Buchanan's Warehouses which were built in 1883–4. Originally Baker's mill and granary they are now desirable waterside residences selling at prices that would trouble the minds of those who worked there not so long ago.

The 'Tower Belle'

Just past the sandwich bar is where the Bristol Packet's river boat, 'Tower Belle' sails from during the summer months.

The 'Tower Belle' was built in 1920 on the Tyne and used as a ferry for the shipyards there. She was originally called the 'Wincombleigh' and after many years of service ended up on the River Thames, where she was renamed and became well known on the Westminster Pier to Greenwich run. In 1977 she was brought to Bristol and now cruises up river to Beese's Tea Garden, the Chequers Inn at Hanham and as far as Keynsham Lock. She also does trips down the Gorge to Avonmouth and the Severn Channel. A lovely boat, she carries on the tradition of the Campbell's pleasure steamers, Albert Head's well-remembered 'Kingstonian' and the 'Penny Steamers' that used to run from St Augustine's Reach before the turn of the century.

Just before you get to Bristol Bridge you will see the

Glass Boat, a most imaginative and pleasing conversion of a barge into a restaurant with a well deserved reputation for excellent food.

Bristol Bridge and Castle Park

It is here that the city of Bristol came into being when an expanding community of Saxons built a wooden bridge across the river. They floated the timber down stream from Kingswood Forest, some eight miles away. The Saxon word for the 'place of the bridge' is 'bricgstow' and it is generally accepted as the original form of the word Bristol.

By 1248 the first stone bridge was completed. It had wooden houses and shops on each side and a chapel dedicated to the Assumption of the Blessed Virgin. The chapel was destroyed by fire in 1642.

As Bristol prospered the bridge became totally inadequate for the volume of traffic. It seems that the roadway dipped in the middle and when waggons passed they leaned towards each other so much that they often got locked together, causing long delays.

In order to increase living space in the cantilevered houses, which were partly built on projecting beams, bow windows were extended out over the water. There were occasions when shipping collided with the bridge and spars and bowsprits crashed through people's sitting windows. Apparently the ground level rooms were extremely cold and in winter the wind blew freely through gaps in the floors causing the carpets of the affluent to rise and fall in a most alarming fashion.

By 1762 the bridge was beyond redemption and demolition commenced. It was during this work that remnants of an ancient and substantial wooden structure were discovered inside one of the piers, thus confirming that a bridge has stood on this site for virtually a thousand years.

The present day bridge was designed by a gentleman with the appropriate name of James Bridges. For several years he suffered the procrastinations of the Bridge Trustees and eventually sailed for the West Indies before the work was even started. Thomas Paty built the bridge and it was opened in 1768 at a cost of £49,000.

It was a beautiful bridge for almost one hundred years until, in 1861, the Corporation set about destroying it in the name of road improvements. The Courtfield stone balustrades and toll booths were removed and girders supported on pillars outside the original piers were inserted to carry a wider roadway. So furious were some citizens that they commenced a Chancery suit against the insensitive Corporation – but to no avail and as recently as 1958 further ugly alterations were made by a city doggedly wrecking itself on account of the motor car.

When the bridge was completed in 1768 the Trustees were empowered to charge tolls to meet the cost of building. By 1793 the public considered the account to be balanced and on September 19th, in a fit of premature enthusiasm, the bridge was thrown open and the toll gates and boards consigned to a celebratory bonfire.

The outraged Trustees (later to be condemned for their 'haughty' attitude) promptly had new barriers erected and announced a continuation of the tolls. Ever given to spontaneous riot, the citizens rose up and the militia came along to suppress them. This situation was repeated on and off for a week until the magistrates, in their wisdom, ordered the soldiers to fire into the crowd and then charge with fixed bayonets. Eleven people died and forty-five were wounded.

By this time public feeling was running so high that the alarmed coroners returned a verdict of 'wilful murder by persons unknown'. This resulted in further rioting and a shower of bricks going through the windows of the Council House and Guildhall. However, tolls were never gathered again at Bristol Bridge – but at what price!

Bristol Castle

Crossing the bridge, you will come to Castle Park which affords several interesting views. This site forms a natural defensive position between the rivers Frome and Avon. It was first occupied by the Saxons who would probably have built some kind of stockade here.

After the Norman Conquest, Geoffrey of Coutance, who was the Bishop of Exeter and a half brother of William I, built a 'motte and bailey' and by the end of the 13th century extensive walls, some twenty feet thick, had been constructed so that the site covered some eleven acres. From the reign of King John to that of Charles I, Bristol was a royal castle and the third largest in the country.

But by 1652 the castle was described as 'having long been in a state of ruin', and in 1656, Oliver Cromell ordered that it be demolished. The little to remain, after local builders had carted away most of the material, was finally destroyed in the bombing raids of 1940–41 – the sad ruins of St Peter's Church having been left as a memorial to the 1,299 people who died in Bristol during that madness.

By the late 19th Century Castle Street had become the main shopping area of Bristol and it was this part of the city which suffered most during the Blitz.

Much of the rubble created by the raids was sent to New York as ballast for the Atlantic Convoy vessels making the return journey to the States. It was used as hardcore for the East River Drive where a plaque commemorates the link between the two cities. There is a copy of this plaque by Neptune's Statue at the head of St Augustine's Reach.

Though long gone, the castle still emanates a presence and should you be passing this way on a misty evening, spare a thought for poor Edward II who was held here before his gruesome death at Berkeley Castle or for the Princess Eleanor who, having been abducted from a ship in the Severn Channel, was confined to the grounds of the castle for forty years and would, no doubt, have spent many lonely hours watching the river flow down to Bristol Bridge. The unfortunate Eleanor is shown on some of the early coats of arms of Bristol.

Finzel's Sugar Refinery

Across the water stands Courage's Brewery. Apparently brewing was taking place on this side of the river as long ago as 1730. In 1788 Philip George established himself on the site with the 'Bristol Porter Brewery'. The beer must have been alright for the steady expansion of George's and now Courage's has taken over and all but obliterated what was once the country's largest sugar refinery.

Conrad Finzel was a native of Frankfurt who had the good sense to desert from Napoleon's army, flee to England and set up a sugar refinery where the brewery now stands.

Sugar refining had been carried on in Bristol since 1616 and the rich rewards of the industry were legendary to the point of the prospering and unrefined 'Bristol Sugar Baker' becoming a standard comic character.

In 1847 a fire destroyed much of Finzel's and the

industrious German then built the most advanced refinery of its period.

You can still see the pennant-stone façade (with filled in windows) of what was the boiler house. At its height Finzel's was processing over 1,200 tons of raw sugar per week and employing some 800 people. In 1881 the refinery went into bankruptcy and the expanding brewery, which now houses the largest mash-tun in the world, steadily took over the site.

The Tramways Generating Station

Going to the far end of Castle Park you will discover a foot-bridge that crosses over the remains of the old castle moat. This takes you to King's Orchard, a modern office development standing on the site of the castle granaries. From here there is a view of the impressive Tramways Generating Station and St Philip's Bridge.

The station was built in 1899 after a lengthy dispute between the Corporation and the Tramway Company. The latter wished to electrify the entire Bristol tram system but the Corporation was out to gain a monopoly of the power supply, even to the point of purchasing the Tramway Company if necessary. Eventually the Corporation, under pressure, gave up on its intentions and the Tramway Company appears to have celebrated by building an unnecessarily flam-boyant power station.

The design is based on a popular pattern used in American cities and space was saved by having the boilers placed above the generating set. Coal was taken up to the boilers by a bucket conveyor system.

By 1938 most of the trams in Bristol had been replaced by buses and the very last of the operation was brought to an abrupt halt on April 10th, 1941 when a bomb hit St Philip's Bridge and severed all the power cables.

St Philip's Bridge

In the 12th century there was a ferry crossing where the new bridge now stands. It was much used by people journeying from Keynsham to Somerset.

In 1837 a company was set up to buy out the ferry, which carried an estimated 100,000 passengers a year. £2,157 was paid in compensation fees and a wooden bridge constructed in 1838. This was replaced by a stone bridge in 1841 which cost £11,000 and, as ever, a toll of one half-penny charged to recover the building costs.

After an outbreak of toll riots, fortunately not so violent as those at Bristol Bridge, the Corporation purchased the site and abolished the charge – but the memory of the toll remains in the local name of 'Half Penny Bridge'. The new bridge was built in 1968.

Returning to Bristol Bridge you will see the towers and church steeples of old Bristol's skyline. Once the tallest buildings of their day, and a cause for wonder, they now are dwarfed by the modern office blocks of the 1960's architectural school of Neo-Brutalism.

Having crossed Bristol Bridge, continue down Welsh Back and turn right into King Street.

King Street and Queen Square

This is perhaps the best preserved street in the centre of Bristol. It was named in honour of the restoration of Charles II. At the docks end of the street are two of the most famous pubs in Bristol.

The 'Old Duke', on your right, was originally named after the Duke of Wellington. However, for many years it has been the bastion of traditional jazz in the West Country and there is live music here every evening and on Sunday lunchtimes. The sign now shows the face of Duke Ellington – a world of difference created by the removal of the letter W.

The Llandoger Trow

Opposite is the Llandoger Trow, a worthy building dating back to 1664. It is not known exactly when Captain Hawkins, who traded from the Welsh Back, opened an inn here naming it after his ship, or trow, which came from the village of Llandogo, just above Tintern on the river Wye.

This pub not only claims – absurdly, to anyone who bothers to read the book – to being the model for the the 'Admiral Benbow' in Robert Louis Stevenson's *Treasure Island* but also the meeting place between Alexander Selkirk and Daniel Defoe.

In 1708 Captain Woodes Rogers equipped two ships, the 'Duke' and the 'Duchess' for a venture to establish "a Trade to the South Seas". Really this meant that jolly old Woodes Rogers was off on a privateering voyage and was selling shares at £103 each to those interested in a little thinly disguised piracy on the high seas. There were plenty of takers.

During the circumnavigation of the world, Rogers rescued Alexander Selkirk from the island of Juan Fernandez where he had been abandoned by his ship after a disagreement with the captain.

On his return to Bristol, Selkirk related his experiences to Defoe who was thus inspired to write the famous tale of *Robinson Crusoe*. This meeting most likely took place on a Sunday because Defoe, like a lot of writers, was in debt and the sabbath was the only day of the week his creditors were not allowed to have him arrested on the street and thrown into gaol.

The Llandoger Trow has played host to many well known actors including Henry Irving, Kate Terry and

Beerbohm Tree. The notorious Judge Jefferies is also said to have stayed here.If he did it is doubtful he approved of the painted ceiling depicting lusty ladies in scant attire. The story goes that when the inn was kept by a particularly merry widow she became so piqued by sailors ogling the ceiling rather than herself that she had the distractions covered with a generous coat of black paint.

The Theatre Royal

Making your way down the street you will pass the St Nicholas with Burton Almshouse which dates back to 1656. You then come to the Theatre Royal, which was designed by Thomas Paty. The foundation stone was laid down in November 1764 and the plans based on the Theatre Royal in Drury Lane, London. The original cramped boxes and balconies still survive. The entrance to the theatre is through the Palladian-designed Coopers Hall, which was converted into the foyer in 1970. The Theatre Royal is the oldest surviving theatre in Britain.

The famous actor, David Garrick, visited the theatre in 1776 and was 'very much pleased', but John Wesley was not as this quote from his letter to the Mayor and Corporation of Bristol indicates – ". . . as most of the present stage entertainments sap the foundations of all religion, as they naturally tend to efface all traces of piety and seriousness out of the minds of men; but they are peculiarly hurtful to a trading city, giving a wrong turn to youth especially, gay, trifling, and directly opposite to the spirit of industry and close application to business; and, as drinking and debauchery of every kind are constant attendants on these entertainments, with indolence, effeminacy, and idleness, which affect trade in an high degree." Obviously John Wesley underestimated the Bristolian devotion to business.

By crossing the road and going down King William Avenue you will have a good view of Queen Square.

Queen Square

In the early 18th century Bristol enjoyed a so-called 'Golden Age' and large parts of the city were transformed as 'new' Georgian buildings replaced the wonderful disorder of the crumbling medieval city.

It is part of Bristol's shame that much of the wealth for this period of development came from an involvement in the Slave Trade.

Ever ambivalent in its attitude to that despicable business, Bristol prospered from the African trade for almost one hundred and fifty years, the only mitigating circumstance for the city being the far greater complicity of Liverpool and London.

In Bristol the slave-trade was something most people regarded with their best blind eye. That it was the pillars of society – mayors, sheriffs, aldermen, merchant venturers and the like – who prospered and did civic good deeds seemed to make the whole thing somehow acceptable.

Certain historians pronounce that such people should only be judged by the moral standards of their own time. What bosh! There was an evil in the city, inspired by greed and the easy money to be made from human suffering.

Needless to say, those who prospered most had little to do with the realities of the 'trade'. They were having a much better time wearing fine clothes and building elegant squares like the one before you.

The north and west sides of Queen Square were mostly destroyed in the Reform Riots of 1831, as was the Mansion House. No 37 was the first American consulate in England. A few of the original Queen Anne houses remain, mostly on the south side of the square and the statue, now stranded in the middle of the road, is of King William III by Rysbrack. It was erected in 1736 and, for reasons ordinary folk might find difficult to understand, shows His Highness all dressed up as a triumphant Roman emperor prancing about on a horse – the undisputed ruler of a traffic island!

Going back to King Street and turning left brings you quickly to the city centre. On the right, just before coming to the main road, there is a fine building, currently Bloomer's restaurant, but originally the first public library in England.

You next come to a pedestrian crossing which will take you to Neptune's Statue at the head of St Augustine's Reach. On the right is a statue of Isambard Kingdom Brunel. It was erected in 1982, which seems a little late in the day to honour the country's greatest engineer and a man who did much of his finest work in Bristol.

St Augustine's Reach and Canon's Marsh

At the head of the Reach stands John Rendall's impressive statue of Neptune. It was moved to this site from the Temple area of the city in 1949 – and is it not a little strange that the marine deity, rather like Bristol itself, has turned his back on the sea; for there he stands, his ancient face turned to the passing traffic.

From here you have the choice of walking down either side of the Reach, or, in the summer months, catching the ferry which will take you back to the Cumberland Basin. Whatever you decide, the commentary continues down the right hand side of the Reach.

The Drawbridges

There was a time when shipping came to the very heart of Bristol, for today's city centre is part of the harbour which has been covered over to create little more than a large roundabout.

In 1714 the first of many bridges was built across the Frome between The Quay and St Augustine's Back.

All known as the 'Drawbridge', each was an attempt to cope with the ever increasing traffic between the two halves of the city. These bridges were a continual cause of frustration because twice a day pedestrians and vehicles were brought to a halt while the bridge was opened to let shipping pass.

In 1893 a fixed bridge was built and progressively

this section of the harbour was covered over to form the gardens and roads as you now see them, the last work being done in 1938.

In 1739 Alexander Pope visited Bristol and was moved to write – ". . . in the middle of the street as far as you can see, hundreds of ships, their masts as thick as they can stand by one another, which is the oddest and most surprising sight imaginable. This street is fuller of them than the Thames, and at certain times only the water rises to carry them out, so that at other times, a long street, full of ships in the middle, and houses on both sides, looks like a dream." A dream sadly lost.

St Augustine's Reach

Pope was writing of the Reach, which, in his day was something of a national wonder.

It was even more of a wonder in the 13th century, for the project involved digging out a channel 18 feet deep, 120 feet wide and 2,400 feet long. This massive undertaking was achieved in eight years with little more than shovels and human muscle. Spade labourers worked for two pence a day, the rate being a half pence a day extra during the winter months, when a man was often expected to work up to his waist in foul and freezing mud. Finally the 'Great Trench' was completed at a cost of £5,000 and it has to be regarded as one of the earliest municipal efforts for the improvement of the port. This extraordinary work was completed in 1247.

For the next three centuries the Port of Bristol flourished but little more was done to improve the quay and most of the merchants seemed quite content to use their own private landing stages rather than invest in further developments.

Their attitude is well summed up by one of those quaint little bits of historical knowledge that some

The Watershed walkway, with stalls, shops and restaurants.

how survive the passage of time. In 1577 it was noted that the churchwardens of St Stephen's were paid for a tombstone that was used to patch up a part of the quay wall. This would not have been an uncommon use for old tombstones in those days.

Dean's Wharf

The cafe and shops on Dean's Wharf, mostly referred to as the 'Watershed' these days, are housed in old transit sheds. The first one, E Shed, is rather grand and was designed by Edward Gabriel in 1894. It has an ornamental frontage looking out towards the city centre, mostly to create a pleasing sight for visitors making their way up Park Street.

The sheds had electrically operated cranes on the roof for unloading shipping that continued to arrive here until the mid 1960's.

Narrow Quay

On the opposite side of the Reach very few of the old warehouses remain. Broad Quay House stands on the site of the old Co-op building, an amazingly Edwardian construction that was pointlessly demolished in the mid 1970's. It seems the current craze for dockside development is mostly about removing old warehouses and replacing them with buildings that look suspiciously like warehouses but are usually insurance offices in disguise.

Broad Quay is absolutely typical of corporate dockside enhancement. It has almost nothing to show of Bristol's eight hundred years of maritime history and with the Unicorn Hotel as a centre piece it has virtually lost its identity – yet this was the very middle of the country's second busiest port two hundred years ago.

There was some excitement along the Reach in 1983 when the China Clipper Society brought its two square-riggers, the 'Inca' and the 'Marques' here for a refit. Suddenly the quay was a muddle of ropes, spars and piles of wood, the air smelt of tar and there were men shaping baulks of timber with adzes. The scene

The Arnolfini arts complex.

was such that every day groups of fascinated people stood about, probably longer than they intended, watching a world which disappeared over a century ago. It was better than the cinema. It was real. Then the ships sailed and Narrow Quay, briefly revitalised, returned to its more usual state of blandness.

Tragically the 'Marques' sank, with the loss of

nineteen lives, off Bermuda the following year.

At the end of the quay stands Bush House, one of the first sensitive conversions of warehousing around the docks. Originally built as a tea store in 1830, it now houses the Arnolfini arts complex. The statue on the point of the quay is of John Cabot looking thoughtfully down the harbour in the direction of his famous journey.

Canon's Marsh and Mardyke Wharf

Once clear of the converted transit sheds you come to Canon's Marsh, an area which, at the time of writing, is being developed to include the European headquarters of Lloyds Bank.

The 'Lochiel', now a floating pub and restaurant, started life as a ferry serving the Western Isles off the coast of Scotland. She was launched in 1939 and continued working until 1970. Her name comes from Loch Eil in Inverness-shire.

Making your way along Canon's Marsh Wharf you will see a round, stone built tower with a weather vane perched rather incongruously on its top. The tower was the base for a steam crane. It was a very busy crane, for although there is little sign of it today, this was an extremely active part of the docks in the early years of the 20th century, because to the right stood the Canon's Marsh Goods Depot, built in 1906, to receive cargoes almost straight from the ships. Also here were the recently demolished Tobacco Bonds built by Cowlins in the 1920's and a once familiar sight to anybody who knows the docks.

More often than not you will find the Wessex Water Authority ship 'Glen Avon' moored here. This vessel

A lugubrious John Cabot ponders the changing face of the city's waterfront.

is an effluent carrier. Fortunately she does not load up in the docks but at the 'sludge jetty' some two miles from Avonmouth. She then makes her way down the Channel to what is described as an 'ecologically safe spot', not far from Ilfracombe, where she off-loads her questionable cargo.

A little further on you come to the quayside base of Square Sail, a company which converts ships and barges for sail training and for use by the film industry. Square Sail owns several vessels and when they are moored here they can create a deceptive atmosphere, especially at night.

The Bristol Gas Company

You next come to the site of the old Canon's Marsh Gas Works.

In 1811, Mr Briellat, a dyer in Broadmead, illuminated his shop and part of the street with gas. His enterprise appears to be the first experiment in street lighting of which there is any local record.

By 1820 the Bristol and Clifton Oil Gas Company was established here. This new company was not allowed to use coal to make gas because the Bristol Gas Light Company had that monopoly. The Bristol and Clifton Company claimed that oil gas gave four times the light of coal gas and that it was free from 'objectionable impurities'.

In 1853 the companies were amalgamated and by 1908 the Bristol Gas Company had laid 360 miles of mains supply, was hiring out 39,390 gas cookers and illuminating 9,462 public lamps.

There was industrial strife here in 1889 when the stokers, not unreasonably, went on strike for a shorter day of eight hours. The Gas Company imported men from outside of Bristol but the irate stokers saw them off or into the docks and the directors, complaining furiously about police apathy, were forced to accept their demands. However, the directors later comforted themselves by putting up the price of gas.

Rounding the corner into Gas Ferry Lane you will find yourself plunged into an environment almost totally unchanged since those days.

When you get back to this century by coming to Anchor Road, turn left and join the Hotwell Road, This will quickly bring you to Mardyke Wharf which has recently been paved and makes a pleasant walkway with views across the water to the ss Great Britain and the marina at Albion Yard.

The Bethel Ship

The 'Bethel' ship was moored here until the late eighteen hundreds. The Bristol Seaman's Friend Society and Bethel Union dates back to 1820 when the hulk 'Aristomenes', known as 'The Ark', was fitted out as a floating chapel and moored on the Grove. The congregations were considerable, numbering between 800 and 1,000, mostly sailors but with more than a few interested landsmen.

In 1883 the 'Gloriosa' was purchased and towed from Liverpool in such bad weather that the hawser parted and the hulk was left to her fate. However, she survived and was taken to the Isle of Man before eventually arriving in Bristol. For many years she was moored at Mardyke, where, on Sunday mornings hundreds of sailors were to be heard bellowing out songs of praise before making their way to one or the other of the forty-two pubs then to be found between Bristol Cathedral and the Hotwell House on the Portway.

The Mardyke

Mardyke Wharf takes its name from the Dutch town of Mardyke and is remembered here because two ships were fitted out by Bristol to take part in the invasion of the Dutch coast ordered by Oliver Cromwell. When you get to the end of the wharf you will come to Michael's restaurant and the dingy flight of steps here lead to the ferry stage.

Assuming you started walking from the Cumberland Basin, this seems a good spot to rest the legs by taking the ferry to the Pump House, for the rest of Hotwells Road has little to offer from the land. Of course, during the winter months you have no choice but to continue down the road and then bear left into Merchants Road which leads to the Cumberland Basin.

Mardyke Wharf to Cumberland Basin

Aboard the ferry you first pass Poole's Wharf. In 1786 a spring was discovered behind the 'Tennis-Court House' near the Mardyke ferry. The owner promptly built a Pump House next to the spring, obviously anxious to profit from the already established trade of the Hotwell Spa's efficacious waters. By 1810 the site was converted into Poole's Mineral Spa Coal Wharf.

Today the wharf is used by the sand boats, which, with luck, will be arriving, departing, or unloading as you pass.

These ships work tidally, making their way down the Avon and into the Channel where they dredge up sand – the Harry Brown can load 650 tons in less than half-an-hour. The ships are off-loaded by the last working cranes in the docks and the whole operation here is much cared for by Bristolians, many of whom regard the sand fleet as a final, if somewhat rusty, reminder of the city's maritime history.

Sometimes, on the hot Sundays of a good summer, the local kids play in the sand dunes piled up on Poole's Wharf and then cool off by diving into the harbour from the bows of the sand boats. This, of course, is not permitted by the powers that be who have long attempted to prevent swimming in the docks.

In 1822 the Dock Company was most anxious to stop the "indecent and improper bathing" taking place in the harbour and to forbid anyone to "undress himself on the shore or expose his naked body to public view." Despite their efforts local folk continued to hurl themselves into the 'noxious' waters and the Leander Swimming Club, in the 1880's, braved both sewage and tide for the annual race down the New Cut from Bath Bridge to Rownham Ferry, which was just outside the Entrance Lock.

Rownham Mead and the Great Dock

After the sand wharf comes a development of new and expensive houses. This is Rownham Mead, which stands on the site of the Great Dock, which was filled in in 1966.

In 1765 William Champion constructed a wet dock here which was able to accommodate thirty-six ships. The cost of the work drove Champion to bankruptcy and in 1770 the site was purchased by the Society of Merchant Venturers and became known as Merchants Dock. Business was not as good as hoped for and in 1796 the Society sponsored an Act of Parliament 'to remove the danger of fire amongst ships in the Port of Bristol'. This lawfully prevented the landing of any inflammable cargo except at Merchants Dock, where the harbour dues happened to be far greater than any other part of the port.

Rownham Mead houses and the former pump house, now a waterside pub.

In the following year a shadowy character by the name of 'Jack the Painter' took to arson with a vengeance, burning ships and warehouses and generally 'frightening the people out of their senses'. In a more questioning age it is difficult to dismiss the notion that Jack was not in the pay of those with a vested interest. Whatever, the Society's business at Merchants Dock picked up quite nicely after this outburst of incendiarism, for which the culprit was later hanged in Portsmouth.

Alighting at the Pump House brings you back to Thomas Howard's Junction Narrows and the Cumberland Basin. However, if the legs are still willing, there is much to be gained by walking only a short distance further.

The Hotwell Spa

Keeping the Cumberland Basin to your left and following the main road past the Entrance Lock, you will notice a bust of Samuel Plimsoll casting a watchful eye down river. You will then come to the remains of the passenger staging used by Campbell's paddle steamers. On your left stands the Colonnade and directly ahead a most impressive view of Brunel's brilliant Suspension Bridge.

The Colonnade is all that remains of the once fashionable Hotwell Spa, the rise and fall of which were both remarkably rapid.

Known to mariners for centuries, the original spring poured out fresh water at the rate of sixty gallons a minute some ten feet above river level at low tide. At high tide the spring was covered by the not over-pleasant waters of the Avon. At a temperature of 76°F, the water could hardly be described as 'hot', nevertheless, the misnomer remains.

The first recorded mention of the spring comes from the 15th century gad-about and early travel writer, William Worcester. He described a fountain which was 'warm as milk' and like the water of Bath.

In 1643 a young army officer wrote of his descent to the spring down a 'steep-winding and craggy way of neere 200 slippery steps' where he found the water 'gushing and pouring out of a mighty stony rocke.'

By 1662 the spring water had been pronounced as 'sovereign for sores and sickness' and the enthusiastic Dr. Venner declared the water to be most beneficial for those suffering from hot livers, feeble brains, and red pimply faces.

By the turn of the century it seems the 'Famous Bristol Hotwell Water' cured everything from hang-overs to acne.

In 1696 the Hotwell House was built on a small promontory jutting out into the river. A special foundation was constructed for the Pump Room so the spring water could be raised thirty feet. There were valves in the pipes that allowed excess well-water to drain back into the river but remained shut against the high tides. Unfortunately these valves were far from foolproof and the spring water often remained fouled by the river for some time after the tide had fallen.

Nevertheless this tainting of the water did little to dissuade the fashionably ailing from drinking gallons of the stuff in the name of good health.

The Hotwell House, as you can see, must have commanded spectacular views of the Gorge and when royal patronage occurred in the form of Catherine of Braganza, a glittering future was assured for this most unlikely of health resorts.

Over the years such worthies as Cowper, Pope, Addison, Sheridan and the Duchess of Marlborough came here to see and be seen. There were subscription balls in the Pump Room and horse racing on the Clifton Downs. Just across the river there was open countryside where pic-nics with fresh strawberries could be enjoyed – and always there was the facinating round of new gossip and deliciously shocking scandal.

Some even found time to sip the efficacious water and, indeed, there were cures, but one is left wondering if they were not more due to an agreeable and active life-style during the 'season' than the properties of the

water described by Alexander Pope as being too hard for the laundress and best used in making tea.

One of the most charming events in all this engaging pursuit of health must have been those river trips when a second boat with musicians on board was chartered to accompany the passengers on their journey down the Gorge, their peaceful progress made all the more wonderful for live music echoing from the cliff face.

And while all this was going on the river remained busy as the larger sailing ships were towed to the Port of Bristol by teams of six or eight rowing boats and the Welsh 'trows' and many other vessels went about their business.

On November 1st 1755 an event occurred which substantiated the claims that the spa water was 'influenced to an unusual degree by the subterranean fire of the earth, and has an evident sympathy with volcanic agencies' – for suddenly the water ran red as blood and could not be drunk.

For the mystified invalids and socialites witnessing this extraordinary occurrence there was no satisfactory explanation until news finally arrived in Bristol of the devastating earthquake that had wrecked half of Lisbon on the same day.

The fame of the spa continued to spread and the 'Bristol Hotwell' season became so established that the Pump Room appointed William Pennington Esq as Master of Ceremonies, giving him a gold medallion on a blue sash to proclaim the extreme dignity of his office.

Dr Carrick, a physician in Clifton, has left behind an excellent description of the spa at this time. 'It was during the summer one of the best frequented and most crowded watering-places in the kingdom. Scores of the nobility were to be found here every season, and such a crowd of invalids of all ranks resorted to the waters that it was often difficult for them to provide themselves with any sort of lodgings. A considerable number of lodging-house keepers had in the course of a few years realised very handsome fortunes without any complaints of extortionate extractions. Three extensive taverns were constantly full and two spacious ballrooms were profitably kept open. There was a well-attended ball, a public breakfast, and a promenade every week, and often twice a week. The Pump Room was all day long the resort of invalids who left with the keeper of the Well many hundreds a year in voluntary donations, and from 12 to 2 o'clock it was generally so crowded that there was often some difficulty in getting up to drink the water. The adjoining walk, (the Colonnade), was filled with fashionable company; the sublime scenery of the cliffs was enlivened by the sounds of music. The Downs and all the avenues to the Hotwell were filled with strings of carriages and with parties on horseback and on foot.'

Thus the elegant terraces and crescents of Clifton and Hotwells came into being and the local populace prospered by renting out almost everything from rooms to wicker-covered wheelchairs.

Among the many testimonials to the curative properties of the water one of the most pleasing is that of Mr. Eaglestone, of College Green, who witnessed Mr. Ralph Millard from London make such a miraculous recovery that he was able to lift a barrel of ale up several steps, within a couple of weeks of not being able to 'scramble to his bed without help'. The invigorated Mr Millard then rode back to London in two days, where he happened to be an innkeeper and no doubt something of an expert in the handling of beer barrels.

Ironically it was the sad belief, held by many of the terminally ill, in the curative powers of the water that lead to the decline of the spa.

That these unfortunates even came to the Hotwell says little for the professional honesty of their physicians who obviously disliked parting with a patient while the least chance of a cure remained, but, when all was lost, packed the hopeless cases off to Bristol, thus avoiding the embarrassing business of having them die while under treatment.

So common were these patients, mostly incurable consumptives, that one terrace of boarding houses became known as 'Death Row'. Gradually the once gay Hotwell Spa took on a sinister reputation.

As popularity declined and charges rose, Dr Carrick wrote again of the spa in 1816, only thirty years after his original and enthusiastic description. 'It has the silence of the grave, to which it seems the inlet. Not a carriage to be seen once an hour, and scarcely more frequently does a solitary invalid approach the neglected spring. One of the ballrooms and taverns has long been shut up, and the other with great difficulty kept open. The lodging-houses, or such of them as still remain open, are almost entirely empty in summer, and not very profitably filled even in winter.'

In 1822 the Hotwell House was demolished. But at the same time the robust Mr. James Bolton attempted to revive the spa by building a new Pump Room in the Tuscan style. It adjoined the Colonnade, standing where the traffic now thunders past.

Bolton was a keen businessman in the Bristol tradition. He charged three pence a glass for the water – which meant taking the 'cure' could cost up to three shillings a day. The only folk not liable for this excessive charge were the paupers who were allowed to draw water from the 'free' tap which stood in the backyard of the new building. Perhaps this notion of a welfare state was too much for the harassed Mr. Bolton, for in 1831 the tap was removed, not being reinstated until 1837, and then only as the result of threatened legal action.

As things went from bad to worse, Bolton augmented his dwindling income by boldly advertising a bizarre range of products which included oiled silk caps and respirators, foreign cigars, umbrellas, fossils available in their natural state or in the form of inkstands and shawl pins, Kent's patent knife-cleaning machines, the 'celebrated' Hotwell toothpowder, health-giving lozenges, boomerangs and a range of dubious sounding 'flesh rubbers'. In fact almost everything a terminal invalid might require.

Despite all his efforts, Bolton's attempt to revive the spa failed and in 1867 the Pump House was demolished to improve the approach of shipping into Thomas Howard's new Entrance Lock.

Only the traffic-embattled Colonnade remains as a gentle reminder of a local distinction now vanished. From time to time the main road is closed in order to inspect the cliff face for loose rocks. To be here on such an occasion makes it possible to feel something of the charming, almost hypnotic ambience that was once the famous Hotwell Spa.

Clifton Suspension Bridge

Of course, we all know it was the twin giants Vincent and Goram who cut out the Avon Gorge with their massive pickaxe. The completion of this excellent work, however, left the good folk of Bristol with the problem of how to get from one side of the Gorge to the other.

For many centuries they managed with the Rownham Ferry but in 1753 William Vicks, a wine trader of the city, left £1,000 to the Merchant Venturers with specific directions that it be invested at compound interest until the sum of £10,000 be reached – an amount he hoped would be sufficient to build a bridge across the Avon.

By 1829 the fund had reached £8,000 and the Merchant Venturers announced a competition. Twenty two designs were received and Thomas Telford, (he of the Menai Bridge), was called upon to be judge.

That the elderly Telford eventually rejected the

plans of the twenty-three year old Isambard Kingdom Brunel says many things. Telford seemed obsessed with the notion that a single span of 702 feet could not possibly be safe – the 580 foot span of his Menai Bridge apparently imposing a standard of safety from which he would not be moved.

For one reason or another Telford managed to reject all the other designs and the frustrated Bridge Committee eventually asked him to supply them with a plan of his own.

Telford turned in a design for a three span bridge mounted on collossal, gothic style, piers rising from the bottom of the Gorge. The centre span was to be 400 feet and the estimated cost stood at £52,000 – a sum which would have left poor William Vicks totally bewildered.

Although Telford's bridge would have looked fine by today's standards, there was nothing 'modern' about its appearance at the time and the situation became one of those rare occasions when public opposition was so strong that a major engineering work was brought to an abrupt halt.

Bristol simply did not want Telford's bridge and a second competition was held and, after much deliberation by the new judges, won by a delighted Brunel who wrote to a colleague – "I produced unanimity amongst fifteen men who were all quarrelling about the most ticklish subject – taste. The 'Egyptian' thing I brought down was quite extravagantly admired by all and unanimously adopted; and I am directed to make such drawings, lithographs etc as I, in my supreme judgement, may deem fit; indeed, they were not very liberal with their money, but inclined to save themselves much trouble by placing very complete reliance on me."

At the ceremonial turning of the first sod of earth on July 21st 1831, Sir Abraham Elton said of Brunel – "There goes the man who reared that stupendous

work, the ornament of Bristol and the wonder of the age."

Had Sir Abraham realized the project was going to take another thirty-three years and that Brunel would die from over-work before its completion he might have chosen more cautious words.

By 1843, with both the Clifton and Leigh Woods abutments completed, the public was informed that the £45,000 raised had been exhausted and that another £30,000 was needed to complete the undertaking. This statement of affairs was all but a death warrant for the bridge and from that date virtually all work ceased.

Thus, for many years, the two enormous piers stood grim against the skyline, a strange monument to failure in a city renowned for its wealth.

That it took Brunel's death in 1859 to generate sufficient funds and energy to complete the bridge says little for Bristol at that time.

It was, in fact, the senior members of the Institution of Civil Engineers who formed a company which had "an interest in the work, as completing a monument to their late Friend and Colleague, Isambard Kingdom Brunel, and at the same time removing what was considered a slur upon the engineering talent of the country."

So the "Ornament of Bristol and wonder of the Age" was really an inheritance the city gained from the bold enterprise of others.

It is sad to say that in a life which knew both success and failure on the grand scale, the incompletion of the Suspension Bridge was Brunel's greatest regret. It was his first engineering commission and as a young man he was immensely proud of it.

The Bridge was opened on December 8th 1864, having been tested by a dead weight of 500 tons of stone which caused the centre to subside seven inches and then return to its original level when the load was removed.

Ever happy to attend a good civic bash, the populace of Bristol turned out in full for the opening ceremony.

The *Bristol Daily Post* of December 9th 1864 tells us – "It is difficult to conceive and much more to describe the bustle and crowding that marked the thoroughfares of the City. The people of Bristol seemed to have turned out en masse, whilst their ranks were swelled by the arrival of immense numbers from the surrounding Towns and Villages. We do not think we should over estimate the crowds that were to be found at some one or other point of the City, if we placed the number at

140,000 to 150,000. Flags and banners were displayed in all directions, the Church bells too rang out their joyous music and everybody was decked out in holiday guise."

The Bridge was decorated – "Elegant in the extreme was the ornamentation of the approaches with evergreens, artificial flowers and flags being displayed with the taste that spoke volumes for the care of Lieutenant Jackson and the gardeners of the neighbourhood."

There was a lengthy procession of delegates of the Trade and Friendly Societies which was followed by stirring speeches, particularly on the theme of the Counties of Gloucestershire and Somerset being joined "in social union as enduring as the chains now, for all time, indissolubly link them together." A bonding finally separated by the formation of Avon, a county created by administrators for administrators.

At half-past four precisely there was a banquet given in the Victoria Rooms after which the stuffed dignitaries made their way back to the Bridge for the illuminations conducted by Mr. Phillips of Weston-super-Mare, who did not have a good day for ". . . though successful from a Scientific Point of View the illuminations failed to afford that amount of gratification to the public which had been anticipated, and universal disapprobation seems to have been engendered in all quarters" – which means the crowd booed and bellowed raucously when the brilliance of the electric and magnesium lights fluctuated and finally presented little more than a dim appearance of the Bridge.

At about 9 o'clock the great mass of people began returning to the city and in doing so caused one of Bristol's more memorable traffic jams – "the vicinity of Hotwells was at times entirely blocked by the thousands of persons who thronged the roads. The omnibuses were densely crowded, the passengers on the tops being so densely packed that they ran great risk of being pitched into the road. The narrow bridge over the inlet to the River near Rownham Wharf was blocked at times for ten minutes together, and fortunately for those who crowded it, the structure is a new and substantial one, and has but recently replaced an old and worn-out bridge."

It seems a great shame Brunel was not there to enjoy all this fun and while both he and his bridge have withstood the tests of time, the latter continues to remain incomplete.

Brunel's original intention was for an altogether more artistic appearance in the Egyptian style of architecture. The piers were to be encased in metal embossed with illustrations of the various stages of construction and symbols of the different trades involved in the work and each tower was to be capped with a reproduction of the Sphinx.

Initially this decorative work was estimated at an additional £10,000. Whatever the cost might be today it seems high time for the city to live up to its much pronounced saying by finishing the job 'ship-shape and Bristol fashion.'

Some Dimensions of The Clifton Suspension Bridge

Total Length	1,352 feet.
Total Span	702 feet 3 inches.
Width	31 feet.
Height	245 feet above road level.
Strength of Bridge	7,000 tons.
Total Weight	1,500 tons.

It is interesting to note the main chains of the bridge are some three inches longer in hot weather than they are during a cold winter spell and that the centre can rise and fall as much as six inches with certain temperature variations.

Morbid Interest Section

It is sad to relate that in desperation and loneliness people do throw themselves from the bridge.

The only adult to survive the fall was Sarah Ann Henly, who, at the age of twenty-four, jumped to an intended oblivion in 1885. You will imagine her amazement when she found herself parachuting to safety by virtue of her dress and voluminous petticoats. With an ignominious splodge poor Sarah landed in the copious Avon mud from which she was rescued. Perhaps the journey down was educational for it is certainly gratifying to know that she went on to live a full life, eventually becoming a grandmother.

In 1896 Elsie and Ruby Brown, aged three and twelve, were thrown from the bridge by their father, who was described as suffering from a temporary derangement. Miraculously they survived his murderous intentions and were picked up by a passing pilot boat.

The Clifton Rocks Railway

It is possible to make a rapid but steep ascent to the Bridge but it means crossing the road with extreme caution, for the traffic here displays little regard for pedestrians.

Just past the Colonnade you will see the bricked in archways of the Clifton Rocks Railway. Opened in 1893, this was a four track system with two pairs of cars operating on an hydraulic counter-balance principle.

Promoted by Sir George Newnes in conjunction with his interests in the Clifton Grand Spa and Hydro, (now the Avon Gorge Hotel), this railway was enormously popular with Bristolians and remained in operation until 1934.

The Zig-Zag

Some fifty paces along from the old railway entrance you come to the 'zig-zag', formerly the 'steep-winding and craggy way of neere 200 slippery steps'.

The path lives up to its name and will take you directly, if somewhat strenuously, to Clifton and the Bridge. The climb is most rewarding but should it result in total exhaustion, the Avon Gorge Hotel has a fine patio where one can sip a well-earned drink and enjoy an excellent view, perhaps lingering long enough for the Bridge to be lit up.

The Suspension Bridge is illuminated by 6,000 light bulbs and it is nothing short of spectacular to walk across it after dark, preferably on a balmy summer night – but for those who venture forth in the mad March gales, when the wind screeches and the bridge shudders and grumbles, but never fails, there is always that faint possibility of hearing Isambard Kingdom Brunel, the last Renaissance Man, chuckling quietly at his own genius.

Conclusion

A little more than a decade ago the docks you have just journeyed around stood empty, the wharves deserted, the timber yards and cranes abandoned.

At the time it seemed the City of Bristol had little idea of what to do with the 'historic' harbour, as it now likes to call it. There were even suggestions that the whole thing be filled in with concrete.

Then, in 1970, the ss Great Britain arrived, towed back on a raft from the Falkland Islands in one of the most enterprising salvage operations of that time. But although thousands of people turned out to witness the ship's arrival, the City appeared none too interested and the restoration project was very nearly lost to London.

In 1973 the narrow boat 'Redshank' turned up and started offering trips from Wapping Wharf. Its owner, Nick Gray, soon became well known for his idiosyncratic commentaries and gradually an awareness of the docks as a place of interest began to dawn and the word 'heritage' become all the vogue in the corridors of power.

Sensing a financial future for the docks, proposals were published, committees formed and, true to form, the harbour dues raised by an astonishing 300%.

Seeing which way the wind was blowing, Nick Gray departed in his converted tar-barge, the 'Jolly', preferring the honest business of carrying cargoes of cat litter on the less commercialised waterways of France and Belgium.

Since then the docks have been developed at a rapid pace to the likes of some, the distaste of others, but uniformly beyond the purses of those who used to live and work here.

The harbour is currently enjoying a success that has eluded it for centuries and, ironically, has nothing to do with its origins.

Now, as our local history becomes 'cameoed' between new housing and business developments it is hoped this book will shed a little light on the realities of the past and some of the people who helped create Bristol's Floating Harbour.

Listings

Boat Trips

Name: Bristol and Bath Cruisers.
Address: Phoenix Wharf, Redcliffe.
Telephone: 214307.
Comment: Modern covered boats available for charter, mostly around the docks, with or without food.

Name: Bristol Ferry Boat Company.
Address: Prince Street Bridge, Bristol.
Telephone: 273416.
Comment: Regular ferry service from Easter to September. Boats run between City Centre and Hotwells – including ss Great Britain – seven days a week and between ss Great Britain and Bristol Bridge at weekends and during school holidays. Boats available for one hour tour of the docks, with commentary and for evening tour of dockside pubs.

Name: Bristol Packet.
Address: Wapping Wharf, Bristol.
Telephone: 268157.
Comment: Regular one hour trips on the narrowboat 'Redshank' at 12.00, 2.00, 3.00 and 4.00 during school holidays and weekends from Easter to September. Bar, toilet and good commentary. 'Redshank' is also available for charter for trips around the docks and up river to Beese's Tea Garden and the Chequers Inn at Hanham.
The Bristol Packet also runs the 'Tower Belle' offering regular trips up river and down

stream to Avonmouth. The 'Tower Belle' departs from Bristol Bridge for all public trips and is available for private charter.

Name: Waverley Excursions Ltd.
Address: Gwalia Buildings, Barry Docks, Wales.
Telephone: 0446 720656.
Comment: Runs the 'Balmoral' and the paddle steamer 'Waverley'. Avon Gorge and Channel trips available from Bristol at Easter also during the summer season during July and August.

Car Parks

Name: Canon's Marsh Car Park
Address: Anchor Road, Bristol.
Comment: Pay and Display.

Name: Castle Park.
Address: Wine Street, Broadmead, Bristol.
Comment: Pay and Display.

Name: ss Great Britain Car Park.
Address: Wapping Wharf, Bristol.
Comment: Pay and Display. Coach dropping off point.

Name: Cumberland Basin Car Park.
Address: Cumberland Basin, Bristol.
Comment: Small, but free!

Galleries

Name: Arnolfini.
Address: Narrow Quay, Bristol.
Telephone: 299191.
Comment: Serious contemporary arts. Book shop and Cinema.

Name:	Avon Fine Arts.
Address:	120 St George's Road (Hotwell Rd), Bristol.
Telephone:	213185.
Comment:	Good selection of Bristol Docks prints.

Name:	Ginger Gallery.
Address:	84 Hotwell Road, Bristol.
Telephone:	292527.
Comment:	General selection of prints and paintings.

Name:	Glevum Studio and Gallery.
Address:	Merchants Quay, Bristol.
Telephone:	634680.
Comment:	Contemporary and traditional marine paintings. Summer marine exhibition.

Hotels

Name:	Avon Gorge Hotel.
Address:	Sion Hill, Clifton, Bristol.
Telephone:	738955.
Comment:	Excellent views of Suspension Bridge and Avon Gorge.

Name:	Hilton International.
Address:	Redcliffe Way, Bristol.
Telephone:	260044.
Comment:	Close to St Mary Redcliffe and City Docks.

Name:	Grand Hotel.
Address:	Broad Street, Bristol.
Telephone:	291645.
Comment:	Central for King Street and Bristol Bridge.

Name:	Holiday Inn.
Address:	Lower Castle Street, Bristol.
Telephone:	294281.
Comment:	Close to Castle Park and Bristol Bridge.

Name:	Royal Hotel.
Address:	Next to Bristol Cathedral.
Comment:	Currently under extensive modernisation.

Name:	Unicorn Hotel.
Address:	Prince Street, Bristol.
Telephone:	294811.
Comment:	On dockside close to City Centre.

Leisure

Name:	Baltic Wharf Leisure Centre.
Address:	Cumberland Road, Bristol.
Telephone:	297608.
Comment:	Slipway, dinghy park and hire. Surfboarding. Instruction available.

Name:	Bristol Bridge Boat Hire.
Address:	Welsh Back, Bristol.
Telephone:	268157.
Comment:	Rowing boats for hire by the hour. Some with electric motors.

Name:	The Thekla
Address:	The Grove, Bristol.
Telephone:	293301
Comment:	Evening Theatre and Music Venue

Museums

Name:	ss Great Britain.
Address:	Wapping Wharf, City Docks.
Telephone:	260680.
Comment:	Ridiculous not to visit this wonderful ship.

Name:	Bristol Industrial Museum.
Address:	Princes Wharf, City Docks, Bristol.
Telephone:	299771 Ext 290
Comment:	Fascinating display of the city's industrial heritage from the 18th century to Concorde. The Museum also runs the steam train service on Wapping Wharf and the steam tug 'Mayflower'.

Name:	Maritime Heritage Centre.
Address:	Gas Ferry Road, City Docks, Bristol.
Telephone:	260680.
Comment:	Exhibition of Bristol shipbuilding. Also sells admission tokens for ss Great Britain.

Name:	National Lifeboat Museum.
Address:	Princes Wharf, City Docks, Bristol.
Telephone:	213389.
Comment:	Collection of historic lifeboats.

Name:	St Nicholas Church Museum.
Address:	St Nicholas Street, Bristol.
Telephone:	299771 Ex 243.
Comment:	Exhibition of local and church history. Brass rubbing.

Public Houses

Name:	The Cottage.
Address:	Baltic Wharf, City Docks, Bristol.
Telephone:	215216.
Comment:	Waterfront pub. Food at lunchtime. Outside tables and fine views of Clifton and Hotwells.

Name:	Llandoger Trow.
Address:	King Street, Bristol.
Telephone:	260783.
Comment:	Three bars. Historic interest. Restaurant.

Name:	The Lightship.
Address:	Welsh Back, Bristol.
Telephone:	272402.
Comment:	Food at lunchtime.

Name:	The Louisiana.
Address:	Bathurst Basin, Bristol.
Telephone:	273849.
Comment:	New Orleans theme and creole food.

Name:	Nova Scotia.
Address:	Nova Scotia Place, Bristol.
Telephone:	262751.
Comment:	Food at lunchtime. Outside tables with view of the docks.

Name:	The Old Duke.
Address:	King Street, Bristol.
Telephone:	277137.
Comment:	Food at lunchtime. Famous for live traditional jazz in the evenings and Sunday lunchtime.

Name:	The Ostrich.
Address:	Lower Guinea Street, Bristol.
Telephone:	273774.
Comment:	Food at lunchtime. Sitting out area with view of Bathurst Basin.

Name:	The Pumphouse.
Address:	Merchant's Road, Hotwells.
Telephone:	279557.
Comment:	Food at lunchtime. Outside eating and drinking area by the Junction Lock. Interesting when the sand boats lock out.

Name:	The Sceptre.
Address:	Baldwin Street, Bristol.
Telephone:	265965.
Comment:	Food at lunchtime. Close to Bristol Bridge.

Name:	Hole in the Wall.
Address:	2 The Grove, Bristol.
Telephone:	265967.
Comment:	Restaurant and bars, including the 'spy'.

Restaurants

Name:	Arnolfini.
Address:	Narrow Quay, City Docks.
Telephone:	299191.
Comment:	Food at lunchtime and early evening. Outside eating and drinking by waterfront.

Name:	The Glass Boat.
Address:	Welsh Back, by Bristol Bridge.
Telephone:	290704.
Comment:	Excellent converted barge serving stylish quality meals lunchtime and evening. Private parties catered for.

Name:	Howard's.
Address:	Avon Crescent, Hotwells.
Telephone:	262921.
Comment:	Evenings only. View of Cumberland Basin.

Name:	Le Grand Café.
Address:	Dean's Wharf, City Docks.
Telephone:	214840.
Comment:	Waterfront restaurant. Covered sitting out area.

Name:	Lochiel.
Address:	Canon's Marsh, City Docks.
Comment:	Highland ferry now used as a restaurant. Good parking. Fine views of docks and St Mary Redcliffe.

Name:	Nutt's Landing.
Address:	Wapping Wharf, City Docks.
Telephone:	221480.
Comment:	Restaurant/cafe. Good home cooking on board.

Name:	The Shoots.
Address:	Canon's Road, City Docks.
Telephone:	250597
Comment:	Lunchtime — reservations only. Evenings from 7.00 until late.

Name:	Watershed.
Address:	Dean's Wharf, City Docks.
Comment:	Popular restaurant.

Snacks

Name:	Brunel's Buttery.
Address:	Wapping Wharf, City Docks.
Telephone:	291696.
Comment:	Good value take-away food and coffee. Sitting out area.

Name:	Loafers Sandwich Bar.
Address:	Welsh Back, City Docks.
Telephone:	272240.
Comment:	Tasty take-away sandwiches and coffee.

Name:	Maritime Buttery.
Address:	Wapping Wharf, City Docks.
Telephone:	297010.
Comment:	Good hot and cold food served all year round. Handy for Great Britain and Bristol Packet narrowboat trips.